Han Ola og han Per

PETER J. ROSENDAHL

Han Ola og han Per

A Norwegian-American
Comic Strip

En norsk-amerikansk
tegneserie

edited by/redigert av
JOAN N. BUCKLEY & EINAR HAUGEN

To Karla —
Enjoy the
Scandinavian festival —
and your heritage! Happy 17th Birthday!
Joan N. Buckley

June 28, 1985

UNIVERSITETSFORLAGET
Oslo - Bergen - Stavanger - Tromsø

Instituttet for
sammenlignende
kulturforskning

The Institute for
Comparative Research
in Human Culture,
Oslo

Serie B: Skrifter
LXIX
Peter J. Rosendahl
Han Ola og han Per
Edited by
Joan N. Buckley and Einar Haugen

ISBN 82-00-06741-6
ISSN 0332-6217

Distribution offices:
NORWAY
Universitetsforlaget
Box 2977 Tøyen
Oslo 6

UNITED KINGDOM
Global Book Resources Ltd.
109 Great Russell Street
London WCIB 3NA

UNITED STATES and CANADA
Columbia University Press
136 South Broadway
Irvington-on-Hudson
NY 10533

Cover design: Hilton Grafiske
Layout: Hilton Grafiske
Printed in Norway by
Gjøvik Trykkeri A/S

Ola and Per

(Original printed in *Decorah-Posten,* January 8, 1926, p. 5)

There are two older fellows,
Whom I hold very dear;
The name of one is Ola,
And the other one is Per.
But whether they are real,
I certainly can't say,
I see them just as fantasy,
A dream by night or day.

The roles they play
In our Western Home out here
Are meant to ease and lighten
The burden that you bear.
For most of us can see
That when everything goes wrong,
A little fun and foolishness
Make it easier to get along.

There are some folks among us
Who think that it is bad
For us to laugh and joke,
Instead of looking sad;
But let them live their own way
In sad and solemn tune,
And then let them crawl back
Into their own cocoon.

But we are glad to know
That living here and there
Are little boys or girls
Just waiting for our Per,
And for our Ola, too,
Without a cap, but snug,
Plus poor old Doctor Lars
With his musty, ancient jug.

Peter Julius Rosendahl
(tr. E. Haugen)

Han Ola og han Per

(Trykt i «*Decorah-Posten*» 8. januar 1926, s. 5)

Der er to gamle Gubber,
som jeg holder noksaa kjær;
den ene heder Ola,
og den anden heder Per,
men om de nu er virkelig
det kan jeg inte si,
jeg ser dem kun i Drømme
og blot i Fantasi.

Den Rolle som de spiller
i Vesterheimen her,
det gjøres for at lette
den Byrde, som I bær.
For en ting ved de fleste,
naar alting gaar paa Kant,
At Livet det blir lettere
med lidt Tull og Vaas iblandt.

Dog findes dem iblandt os,
som tror det gaar for vidt,
at se oss dra paa Smilen
og kvikne op en «bit»,
men de maa faa Lov at leve
efter egen Sæt og Vis,
de maa faa Lov at krybe
ind i sin egen «Chrysalis».

Men vi glædes ved den Tanke,
at der findes hist og her
Smaagutter eller Jenter,
som venter paa han Per,
som venter paa han Ola
saa luelaus og tryg,
og den stakkars Dr. Lars'n
med sin gamle mugne «Jug».

Peter Julius Rosendahl

Contents

Innhold

Preface

The popularity of the Norwegian-American comic strip *Han Ola og han Per* by P. J. Rosendahl is attested by its long run and its many reruns among Norwegian immigrants in the United States. What is less understood and appreciated is that for the student of American immigrant life and experience it is also a precious cultural resource. The purpose of this publication is to make its first part available both for American and Norwegian readers and scholars in convenient book form, and by giving it a proper setting through a dual introduction, to bring out its importance (a) as a unique sample of the humor of an important American ethnic group, and (b) as an authentic linguistic document of the daily life of a bilingual community in the process of transition from Norwegian to American identity. The first topic will be introduced by Professor Joan Buckley, the second by Professor Einar Haugen.

The inception of the project goes back to a post-retirement lectureship by Einar Haugen at Concordia College (Moorhead, Minnesota) in 1978, when the two editors discovered their mutual interest in the strip. As a specialist in English, Joan Buckley had been especially interested in the literature of Norwegian-American immigrants. As a specialist in Scandinavian, Einar Haugen had published extensively on the language of Norwegian-American immigrants. Both of them wished to see it made available not only to scholars, but also to general readers in America as well as Norway. This could be done by adding two types of information to the original texts: (a) English translations of the captions and dialogue and (b) Norwegian translations of the many English words and phrases in the dialogue. Both have now been provided beneath the strips: the English dialogue is immediately below the pictures, numbered by frames, while the Norwegian equivalents of the English words are below these again, separated by a line. Each strip is numbered sequentially, after an English caption to the right of the original Norwegian.

The reader will notice that this book contains only 223 of a total of 599 strips, although the introductions refer to many comic strips with a higher number. These have not been selected, but are in fact the first 223 published. While it would have been desirable to print all the strips, the economics of publishing decided us to make a humbler start. If public interest should be such as to demand more, we are sure that a second volume could easily be added. The material is ready.

Research for this book was supported by the National Endowment for the Humanities Summer Seminars for College Teachers, at the University of New Mexico in 1977 and at Ohio State University in 1981. Joan Buckley thanks Hamlin Hill of New Mexico and Patrick B. Mullen of Ohio State for encouragement, and her husband, Wendell D. Buckley, for preparation of the "Order of Publication" bibliography. The editors are also grateful to the following institutions for research assistance: the Anundsen Publishing Company, Decorah, Iowa; the Luther College Library, Decorah, Iowa; Concordia College Ylvisaker Library, Moorhead, Minnesota; the University of North Dakota Chester Fritz Library, Grand Forks, North Dakota; and the Minnesota Historical Society, St. Paul, Minnesota. The Royal Norwegian Ministry of Foreign Affairs, Oslo, Norway, and the administration of Concordia College, Moorhead, Minnesota have also given support which made this study possible. Finally, the editors wish to thank their families for endless patience with "Ola and Per".

J.B.
E.H.

Forord

Den popularitet som den norsk-amerikanske serien *Han Ola og han Per* av Peter J. Rosendahl nøt blant norske utvandrere til Amerika bekreftes ved dens lange liv i *Decorah-Posten* og dens mange opptrykk. Det som vel er mindre kjent og verdsatt er at den også er en umistelig kulturell skatt for alle som interesserer seg for amerikansk immigranthistorie og kulturliv. Meningen med denne utgivelsen er å gjøre en vesentlig del av den tilgjengelig for amerikanske og norske lesere og kjennere i hendig bokformat. Samtidig skulle den få sin bakgrunn og betydning belyst ved innledninger som skal betone dens betydning (a) som et enestående eksempel på humor i en viktig amerikansk etnisk gruppe, og (b) som et autentisk språkdokument fra dagliglivet i et tospråklig samfunn i overgangen fra norsk til amerikansk identitet. Det første emnet blir presentert av professor Joan Buckley, det annet av professor Einar Haugen.

Prosjektets opprinnelse går tilbake til en forelesningsserie av Haugen på Concordia College i Moorhead i Minnesota i 1978, da utgiverne oppdaget sin felles interesse i serien. Som spesialist i engelsk litteratur, hadde Buckley særlig interessert seg for humor, deriblant norsk-amerikansk humor (hun er født Naglestad). Som spesialist i nordisk språk og selv oppvokset i et norsk-amerikansk miljø, hadde Haugen skrevet atskillig om norsk-amerikansk språk. De ønsket begge å gjøre serien tilgjengelig ikke bare til vitenskapsmenn, men også til vanlige lesere både i Amerika og i Norge. Dette krevet at to slags tillegg ble gjort til Rosendahls opprinnelige tekst: (a) en engelsk oversettelse av overskriftene og dialogen, og (b) norske oversettelser av de mange engelske glosene i dialogen. Begge er nå plassert under bildene i serien. Den engelske oversettelse av dialogene er nummerert etter de enkelte bildene, og den norske oversettelsen av de engelske glosene i Amerika-norsken står under en strek nederst på siden. Hver episode er nummerert i orden, etter en engelsk oversettelse av overskriften til høyre for den norske.

Leseren bør være oppmerksom på at vi har tatt med bare 223 av de 599 episodene som Rosendahl tegnet. Innledningene refererer også til dels til senere episoder. Dette er de første 223 episoder som Rosendahl tegnet, i den orden som *Decorah-Posten* trykket dem. En kunne ønske å ha hele serien, men utgiverøkonomi krevet en mindre bok. Hvis det skulle bli et sterkt krav fra publikum om videre utgivelse kan et bind til lett skaffes. Stoffet ligger ferdig.

Støtte til forskning er kommet fra the Humanities Summer Seminar for College Teachers, ved Universitetet i New Mexico i 1977 og Ohio State University i 1981. Joan Buckley takker Hamlin Hill i New Mexico og Patrick B. Mullen ved Ohio State for oppmuntring, og sin mann Wendell D. Buckley for utarbeidelse av den bibliografiske oversikten bakerst i boken. Utgiverne takker også følgende institusjoner for forskningshjelp: Anundsen Publishing Company, Decorah, Iowa; Luther College Library, Decorah, Iowa; Concordia College Ylvisaker Library, Moorhead, Minnesota; University of North Dakota Chester Fritz Library, Grand Forks, North Dakota; og The Minnesota Historical Society, St. Paul, Minnesota. Det kongelige norske Utenriksdepartement, Oslo, og administrasjonen ved Concordia College, Moorhead, Minnesota, har også hjulpet til å gjøre denne forskning mulig. Til slutt vil begge utgiverne takke sine respektive familier for deres uendelige tålmod med «Han Ola og han Per».

J.B.
E.H.

The Humor of *Han Ola og han Per*

Joan Naglestad Buckley

In the Upper Midwest humor lives among the descendants of Norwegian-American immigrants mainly in the tall tales spun by the coffee gang gathered in the small-town corner cafes, in the numbskull riddles and jokes passed on by the teenagers, and in the comic strip *Han Ola og han Per*. Drawn by Peter Julius Rosendahl from 1918 to 1935 for the *Decorah-Posten,* a Norwegian language newspaper, the comic strip was reprinted almost continually until the paper ceased publication in 1972.[1] This comic strip created by a Spring Grove, Minnesota, farmer was one of the *Decorah-Posten*'s most popular features.[2] *Han Ola og han Per* was also unique in the three major Norwegian-American newspapers which led a flourishing immigrant press from the mid-nineteenth to the mid-twentieth century.[3] By 1918 when the comic strip first appeared, the Norwegian-American immigrants constituted an ethnic group, numbering nearly two million, with established traditions and culture predominantly rural. An important recorder of the culture, the newspaper used the comic strip to build and maintain circulation among the Norwegian immigrants. During the 1920's the *Decorah-Posten* reached its top circulation of about 45,000 subscribers, most of whom were midwestern Norwegian-American immigrants and their descendants, but by 1950 the subscribers dropped to about 35,000.[4]

That the Spring Grove, Minnesota, farmer-artist was familiar with the Norwegian-American immigrant culture is evident from his biography as well as from the language and contents of the comic strip. Rosendahl's parents were Paul and Gunhild Rosendahl, early Minnesota pioneers who homesteaded during the early 1850's on a farm southwest of Spring Grove, Minnesota, the oldest settlement of Norwegians in Minnesota. The father, Paul, who emigrated from Hadeland, Norway, distinguished himself by his Civil War service, by being a Register of Deeds for Houston County, and later by being elected to the Minnesota State Legislature. Similarly, Peter Julius engaged in a variety of occupations besides that of cartoonist. Born in 1878, he lived his entire life in his home community, where he attended the public grade school. This rural community in southeastern Minnesota, almost on the Iowa border, was the scene he portrayed in his comic strip. His only formal training in art was a correspondence course from the Federal School of Applied Cartooning at Minneapolis during the years 1919—1920. Not only a farmer and a cartoonist, he wrote poetry and song texts, painted portraits, and made sketches and drawings. He drew many single cartoon-like pictures of personalities, inventions, and objects in addition to his weekly comic strip. A quiet, modest man, he married a second-generation Halling, Otelia Melbraaten, and they were the parents of four children. Rosendahl was not widely traveled, but he revealed his vivid imagination in the ludicrous situations in which he placed his protagonists and in the wild adventures which they survived. During the summer and fall when he was busy with farming, Rosendahl often had his comic strip characters bid the readers "good-bye" until fall. Frequently the readers then wrote letters to the editor to request that *Han Ola og han Per* return. After 1935 Rosendahl could not be persuaded to continue the comic strip. In 1942 he took his own life.[5]

Today *Han Ola og han Per* is significant because it illustrates the traditional primary values of humor: as entertainment, for anyone able to read "Spring Grove Norwegian", which is discussed in Einar Haugen's essay on the language; as literary and graphic artistry; and as history, with predominant folklore elements, which reflects mainly an immigrant society's pains and difficulties of adapting to mainstream America with its rapidly changing customs and attitudes. The artist described the roles played by Ola and Per in helping to lighten the burden in their "Western Home." He claimed:

> When everything goes wrong,
> A little fun and foolishness
> Make it easier to get along.[6]

He explained that people who thought it ridiculous to smile should be permitted to live in their own serious way, but he preferred to know those who eagerly awaited the weekly appearance of Per, Ola, and Dr. Lars with his old musty jug.

Rosendahl's comic characters made their first appearance on Tuesday, February 19, 1918, in the *Decorah-Posten*, and during that year five more comic strips appeared. These were representative in introducing the main farmer protagonists, Ola and Per, who had endless problems in coping with mainstream American life, and in exploring Norwegian-American vernacular. The first strip, ten scenes with captions along the bottom in addition to the dialogue given in the balloons, describes Ola's ride in his new car and the ineptness of his friend, Per, in helping him tame his "cyclone-pet," or in "Spring Grove Norwegian," "Karsen" [the car]. This strip sets the predominant plot pattern of the characters making an attempt to improve their lives, only to have their efforts end in disaster. The slapstick of the old Keystone comedy formula of pies in the face, punches on the

Humoren i *Han Ola og han Per*

Joan Naglestad Buckley

I øvre del av Midt-Vesten blomstrer humoren blant etterkommerne av norsk-amerikanske immigranter. Den gir seg uttrykk på flere måter, gjennom skrønene som oppstår blant «kaffegjengen» som møtes i kaféene på hjørnet i småbyene, i molbogåtene og -vitsene som florerer blant tenåringene, og i tegneserien *Han Ola og han Per*.

Denne serien ble tegnet av Peter Julius Rosendahl for *Decorah-Posten,* en norsk-språklig avis, i årene mellom 1918 og 1935, og ble stadig opptrykt helt til avisen gikk inn i 1972.[1] Tegneserien, som ble skapt av en farmer fra Spring Grove, Minnesota, var et av de mest populære innslagene i *Decorah-Posten.*[2] *Han Ola og han Per* var dessuten enestående i den norsk-amerikanske presse, som hadde sin glansperiode fra midten av det nittende fram til midten av det tyvende århundre.[3] Da tegneserien så dagens lys, dannet norsk-amerikanerne allerede en egen etnisk gruppe på nesten to millioner mennesker med grunnfestede tradisjoner og en kultur som for en stor del var en ren bondekultur. Avisen, som var et betydelig organ for denne kulturen, benyttet tegneserien til å styrke og opprettholde opplagstallet sitt blant norsk-amerikanerne. I løpet av 1920-årene nådde *Decorah-Posten* sitt høyeste opplagstall på ca. 45.000 abonnenter. De fleste av disse var norsk-amerikanske immigranter i Midt-Vesten og etterkommerne deres, men i 1950 hadde opplagstallet sunket til ca. 35.000.[4]

Det er tydelig at bondekunstneren fra Spring Grove, Minnesota, hadde inngående kjennskap til norsk-amerikansk immigrantkultur. Både hans biografi, så vel som språket og innholdet i selve tegneserien bærer preg av dette. Rosendahls foreldre var Paul og Gunhild Rosendahl, som var blant de første Minnesotapionérer. De fikk sin egen nybyggergård sørvest for Spring Grove, Minnesota i begynnelsen av 1850-årene. Dette området er det eldste norske nybyggersamfunn i Minnesota. Faren Paul, som utvandret fra Hadeland i Norge, gjorde seg bemerket ved sin innsats under borgerkrigen, gjennom sitt arbeid som skjøte-registrator (register of deeds) for Houston County (fylkeskommune), samt ved sitt senere innvalg i Staten Minnesotas lovgivende forsamling. Peter Julius, allsidig som sin far, hadde også flere forskjellige yrker og verv ved siden av å skape tegneserier.

Han var født i 1878, og bodde hele sitt liv i hjemkommunen, hvor han gikk på folkeskolen i bygda. Dette bondesamfunnet i sørøstre Minnesota, nesten på grensen til Iowa, er det som blir skildret i tegneserien. Den eneste formelle kunstutdannelse han fikk, var et brevkurs ved Den føderale tegneskolen i Minneapolis i årene 1919—20. Foruten å være bonde og tegner, skrev han også dikt og sangtekster, malte portretter og laget skisser og tegninger. Han tegnet flere karikaturlignende bilder av kjente personer, oppfinnelser og gjenstander, foruten sin faste ukentlige tegneserie. Han var en rolig og beskjeden mann, som giftet seg med en hallingjente av annen generasjon, Otelia Melbraaten. Paret fikk fire barn. Rosendahl var ingen bereist mann, men han røpet sin livlige fantasi i de komiske situasjonene han plasserte personene sine i, og i de utrolige hendelsene som de alltid slapp fra med livet i behold. Om sommeren og høsten, når han var travelt opptatt med gårdsarbeidet, lot Rosendahl tegneseriefigurene sine ta avskjed med leserne fram til høsten. Da hendte det ofte at leserne skrev til redaktøren med bønn om at *Han Ola og han Per* måtte komme tilbake. Etter 1935 var det ikke lenger mulig å få beveget Rosendahl til å fortsette tegneserien. I 1942 tok han sitt eget liv.[5]

Han Ola og han Per har sin verdi også i dag fordi den belyser de tradisjonelle grunnverdiene i enhver form for humor: underholdningsmessig, for enhver som er i stand til å lese «Spring Grove-norsk» (kfr. Einar Haugens essay vedr. språket), litterært og kunstnerisk, og rent historisk. Hovedvekten er her lagt på elementer fra folkelivet, og serien legger særlig vekt på å skildre immigrantsamfunnet og dettes stadig skiftende idéer og holdninger. Kunstneren skildrer Ola og Pers rolle «i Vesterheimen her» ved å legge vekt (som han skrev) på «å lette den byrde som I bær». Når livet er vanskelig, blir det litt lettere å leve «med lidt Tull og Vaas iblandt».[6] Han hevdet videre at mennesker som synes det er synd å smile, bør få leve så alvorlig som de bare vil, men at han selv foretrakk å gledes over dem som hver uke ivrig ventet på at han Per, han Ola og Dr. Lars med «juggen» skulle komme tilbake.

Rosendahls «moromenn» gjorde sin aller første entré tirsdag 19. februar 1918 i *Decorah-Posten.* I løpet av samme år kom det fem episoder til fra hans hånd. Det som særtegner dem er at de innfører hovedpersonene — farmerne Ola og Per — som ustanselig har problemer med å tilpasse seg den amerikanske levemåten og med å finne ut av det norsk-amerikanske dagligspråket. Den første episoden, ti scener, med tekst under i tillegg til dialogene i snakkeboblene, viser Ola på kjøretur i sin nye bil, og vennen Per som uten hell hjelper ham med å temme «syklondyret», eller på Spring Grove-norsk: *Karsen* (the car). Grunntemaet i serien blir fastslått allerede i denne episoden: personenes mislykte forsøk på å mestre tilværelsen, og de knall og fall som disse forsøkene alltid ender med. Slapstickstilen à la Keystone

nose, and falls in the mud characterized the series from the beginning.

The second strip, printed in seven vertical scenes on April 16, 1918, depicts the good neighbors' attempt to capture a skunk by following the instructions given in an English book which they had to interpret in Norwegian. Of course, something went wrong, and Ola hit Per instead of the skunk. This second strip also reveals that the series was used to solicit readers for the *Decorah-Posten*, for where else had the characters read that that newspaper offered five dollars for one skunk skin? Ola and Per decide to complain to the newspaper about the kind of fool who prints such misleading information. This second strip also sums up the philosophy of the series in the biblical saying that "the last will be worse than the first."

The third strip, three vertical scenes, published April 26, 1918, describes kind-hearted Ola's hypocritical sadness at Per's mistreatment of the pigs and the cow's contentment with Ola's fine care. This contrast of the highfalutin person who cannot carry out simple tasks with the common man who shows sensitivity in caring for creatures, and furthermore even with the animals that talk and express emotions, is basic to the series and well rooted in the native American humor tradition.

The last three strips of the first year continue these features while the artist was experimenting with format and developing the characters and situations. The fourth comic strip, which was nine scenes in length (*Decorah-Posten,* 28 May 1918), mocks Per's pretensions to success as a lover. Foiled by the girl's parents when he attempts to sneak into her bedroom by crawling up a ladder, Per at first blames the unpredictability of women as the cause of his misfortune but in the last frame, he wisely admits he had only himself to blame. This strip, incidentally, alludes to a well-known rural Norwegian custom known in New England as bundling.

The fifth strip, three large vertical scenes (2 August 1918), makes fun of the protagonists' inability to put a ring in the nose of the huge hog that Per owns. The beast bests them both and gives Per quite a ride on the hog's back while Ola hangs on to the hog's tail for dear life. Throughout the series animals outwit humans frequently, thereby suggesting the superiority of the animal to the human world.

The last strip of the year, a "drama in four acts" (13 December 1918), shows Ola being whacked by Per when he tries one of Per's inventions for slaughtering the hog that, of course, goes free. All these comic strips expose the world as being other than what it seemed to be. The implication is that since the universe was believed to be orderly or purposeful and man a rational creature, deviations from these standards were ridiculous. In this last strip the format changed; the captions disappeared and the four panels were published horizontally in double-decker fashion at the bottom of the page.

When the comic strips resumed publication in the *Decorah-Posten* on January 9, 1920, after the appearance of only one strip in 1919, the title, *Han Ola og han Per,* was used for the first time. But the next five strips returned to the vertical format. With the placement of the entire comic strip horizontally on April 30, 1920, the customary format of four panels across the bottom of the page, usually on page three in the Friday edition of the paper, began. The standard size and length of the comic strips were retained throughout the publication of the strips until they ceased their original run on July 19, 1935.

The "Ola and Per" series came into being slowly, and during the first four or five years it did not have the continuity it later developed. Usually during each year, too, the readers could count on Ola and Per's taking a vacation. This event was announced by a special ad in the *Posten*, and their return was heralded by sneak previews weeks in advance so that new subscribers could catch their first re-appearance. When Per and Ola returned to the newspaper, they always came back home to the vicinity of Decorah, Iowa, since most of the subscribers were familiar with the "home town." The only drawing of this city nestled among the hills (348) seems to be authentic.

Rosendahl's creation fits in well with the historical development of the comic strip in America as it changed during the 1920's and 1930's from broad slapstick to the family funnies and later the adventure comic strip. The antics of Ola and Per suggest the "fall guy/straight guy" of gag and slapstick humor, as in Bud Fisher's *Mutt and Jeff* (1907). Then the family situation in the comics expanded between World War I and the Depression. As Sidney Smith's *The Gumps* (1917) and Frank King's *Gasoline Alley* (1918) showed the growth of a typical urban American family, *Han Ola og han Per* depicted the Norwegian-American immigrant family in its rural setting. Other influences appear in the antics of the American-German twins, Hans and Fritz, in Rudolph Dirks' *The Katzenjammer Kids,* and in the marital escapades of Maggie and Jiggs in George McManus' *Bringing Up Father* (1913). Then beginning in 1922 adventures dominated *Han Ola og han Per* as Ola and Per took trips to Africa, Siberia, the North Pole, and tropical

— bløtkaker i fjeset, nesestyvere, sølepytthumor — kjennetegner serien helt fra første stund. Den neste episoden som ble trykt i syv vertikale bilder den 16. april 1918, skildrer de gode naboers forsøk på å fange en skunk (stinkdyr) ved å følge instruksjoner i en engelskspråklig bok som de først må oversette til norsk. Det går selvfølgelig galt, og ender med at Ola treffer Per istedenfor skunken. Episoden røper dessuten at tegneserien ble brukt til å lokke lesere til *Decorah-Posten*, for hvordan kunne ellers skikkelsene vite at avisen tilbød fem dollars for et skunkeskinn? Ola og Per vil klage til avisen: hva for en tosk var det som kunne sette en så villedende opplysning på trykk? Denne episoden summerer også opp seriens visdom: bibelsitatet om at «det siste vil alltid bli enda verre enn det første».

Den tredje episoden, tre vertikale bilder trykt 26. april 1918, skildrer den godhjertede Olas hyklerske sorg over at Per vanskjøtter grisene sine. Samtidig ser vi hvor fornøyd Olas egen ku er over det gode stellet den får. Kontrasten mellom den høyttravende personen som ikke klarer å utføre de enkleste praktiske gjøremål, og den enkle mann som viser følsomhet overfor dyr, og attpåtil dyr som kan snakke og uttrykke sine følelser, er en grunntanke i serien og rotfestet i tradisjonell amerikansk humor.

De samme idéene kommer tilbake i de tre siste episodene dette året, mens kunstneren selv er opptatt med å eksperimentere med formatet og videreutvikle skikkelsene og hendelsene. Den fjerde episoden som består av ni scener (*Decorah-Posten*, 28. mai 1918), driver gjøn med Pers forsøk på å opptre som beiler. Men pikens foreldre hindrer ham akkurat idet han skal til å klatre inn i soverommet hennes. Per gir først de upålitelige kvinnene skylden for uhellet, men i siste bilde innrømmer han klokelig nok at han bare har seg selv å takke. Denne episoden hentyder ellers til den velkjente norske bondeskikken med nattefrieri.

Den femte episoden, tre vertikale scener (2. august 1918) gjør narr av at personene ikke klarer å sette ring i nesen på en stor purke som Per eier. Dyret har dem begge til beste og gir Per en dyktig kjøretur på griseryggen mens Ola klynger seg til griserumpa for sitt bare liv. Gjennom hele serien utkonkurrerer dyrene menneskene ofte, noe som antyder at dyreverdenen er menneskeverdenen overlegen.

Den siste episoden dette året (13. desember 1918), et «drama i fire akter», viser Ola som får en kilevink av Per når han prøver en av griseslakteroppfinnelsene hans, som selvfølgelig fører til at grisen slipper unna. Alle disse episodene viser at verden ikke er slik den burde være. Den underliggende tanke er at ettersom universet etter sigende er både velordnet og meningsfylt og mennesket et fornuftsvesen, er alle avvik fra denne grunntanken laterlige. I den siste episoden er formatet endret, tekstrammene er borte og de fire bildene er trykt horisontalt i «to etasjer» nederst på siden.

Da tegneserien kom tilbake til *Decorah-Posten* den 9. januar 1920, etter at bare en eneste episode var kommet i løpet av 1919, ble tittelen *Han Ola og han Per* benyttet for første gang. De fem neste episodene var nå igjen trykt i vertikalt format. Da hele serien ble trykt horisontalt den 30. april 1920, ble det vanlige formatet, fire bilder på tvers over nederste del av siden, innledet. Standardstørrelsen og -lengden ble fra nå av bevart gjennom hele seriens levetid, helt til siste dag, den 19. juli 1935.

Ola og Per-serien hadde en langsom fremvekst, og de fire-fem første årene den eksisterte hadde den ikke samme kontinuitet som den senere oppnådde. Vanligvis kunne leserne regne med at Ola og Per tok ferie en gang i året. Ferien ble varslet i en egen annonse i *Posten,* og hjemkomsten ble gjort kjent ved hjelp av «snikomtale» flere uker i forveien. På den måten kunne nye abonnenter følge med fra starten av. Når Per og Ola kom tilbake til avisen, kom de alltid tilbake til Decorah-området i Iowa, ettersom de fleste abonnenter var kjent med «hjembyen». Den eneste tegningen som finnes av denne byen (348), omgitt av åser, er antagelig autentisk.

Rosendahls verk er symptomatisk for tegneseriens historiske utvikling i Amerika og de endringer som fant sted i løpet av 1920- og 1930-årene, fra bredpenslet slapstick via familieunderholdning og senere til spenningseventyrene. De krumspring og eventyr som Ola og Per kommer ut for, er i tråd med «slem gutt-/snill gutt»-stilen fra vitser og slapstickhumor, slik som f.eks. Bud Fishers *Mutt and Jeff* (1907). Deretter hadde familiescenene sin store glansperiode mellom 1. verdenskrig og depresjonen i 30-årene. Samtidig som Sidney Smiths *The Gumps* (1917) og Frank Kings *Gasoline Alley* (1918) viser fremveksten av den typiske amerikanske byfamilien, fremstiller *Han Ola og han Per* norsk-amerikanske immigranter i landlige omgivelser. Andre påvirkninger stammer fra de tysk-amerikanske tvillingene Hans og Fritz (Knoll og Tott) og skøyerstrekene deres i Rudolph Dirks *The Katzenjammer Kids*, og fra ekteskapsviderverdighetene hos Maggie og Jiggs (Finbeck og Fia) i George McManus' *Bringing Up Father* (1913). Fra 1922 var det spenningseventyrene som dominerte hos Ola og Per. Nå drar de på tur til Afrika, Sibir, Nordpolen og sydhavsøyene. Denne forandringen har sitt sidestykke i den utvikling som tegneseriene

islands. This change is parallel to the change that came to comic strips with the adventures of Roy Crane's *Wash Tubbs* in 1924, George Storm's *Phil Hardy* and *Bobby Thatcher* in 1925—27, and Harold Gray's *Little Orphan Annie* of 1924 which introduced exotic adventures with homespun right-wing ideas.[7] Also, *Han Ola og han Per* followed the custom of the early comic books which appeared as reprint collections of favorite comic strips. Beginning in 1921, Rosendahl's comic strips were reprinted in eight volumes which were intended as "come on" premiums for subscribers to the *Decorah-Posten*.

The family nature of the first years of *Han Ola og han Per* is in keeping with the tradition of Norwegian-American immigrant literature to depict the immigrant in relation to his family — for the main motive for the Norwegian immigrant was a better life not just for himself but for his whole family. The cast of characters for the Ola and Per comics includes their relatives. The six main characters are Ola, Per, Lars (Per's brother), Polla (Per's wife), Værmor (Per's mother-in-law), and Dada (the child of Per and Polla). Most of the strips focus on Ola and Per but frequently a series features one of the other characters, and sometimes the characters play supporting roles or serve as foils to Ola and Per. Several times Ola's wife, Mari, enters, but she is usually said to be on her way to Minneapolis or Norway. Each of these characters is delightful mainly because each embodies incongruous traits and contradictions.

With Ola and Per as the center, the strips show two neighbors who go through an endless variety of experiences with one or the other coming up with some fantastic new idea. As the center of his family, Per is possibly the main protagonist. He is drawn as the tall, long-legged, full-bearded character who always wears his Prince Albert coat tails and his derby hat. In spite of his cultured appearance, he usually has a tool in his hand. His genius is coming up with new patents that make the farm family more dependent upon mechanical devices, possibly thereby reflecting Rosendahl's own interest in new inventions and certainly doing for rural life what George Derby's and Rube Goldberg's inventions did for the urbanite. These patents, however, serve mainly to complicate daily living, and their use results in chaos. But Per is no more successful as a Casanova. Once married to Polla and the father of Dada, he then assumes the role of head of the house who has the authority to make decisions, even though some of those decisions are forced on him by others. As the authority on inventions as well as family, Per plays the braggart or *alazon* role.

Ola is the good neighbor-farmer who offers friendly, free advice or seeks a solution from "Mr. Know-How" to one of his problems. Ola is the *eiron* character who remains quiet until his advice is needed or he needs assistance. Always bare-headed, he is short of stature, usually wears farmer's overalls, and often appears with his pitch-fork over his shoulder. Some of his main problems of coping appear to be caused by his lack of mechanical aptitude or at least unfamiliarity with operating mechanical devices. His consultations with Per often result in chaos, however, so that usually Per is the victim and Ola gets the last laugh, but sometimes Ola becomes a victim or they both are (23—25).

The main representative of the newcomer to America is Per's brother, Lars, who has been "educated" at both Oslo and Berlin. His role is clearly that of the "learned fool." His first reaction when he arrives on the scene from Norway is shock at the speed here (20). From then on, Lars is bounced from one shock to the next as he becomes involved in the most weird situations imaginable. He is often given tasks for which he says he knows "exactly what to do," but since he goes ahead without knowing anything about the chore, the situation can only end in disruption. His distinguished appearance — he has an exceptionally long, narrow beard and always wears his black top coat with matching stovepipe hat — hides his naiveté and lack of common sense. When he cannot cope with rural America any longer, the wise fool decides to go to China because he has heard that there one man could have several wives. En route he writes Per from Hollywood saying that he has accepted a post as a missionary there because he feels he can use his seven years of religious training to help so many "ungodly attractive" girls (101). His religious work ends quickly, however, probably because he has a constant craving for "home-brew." Seldom separated from his jug, Lars often shows the effects of inebriation. When he returns from New York, where he studied to be a chiropractor, he is soaked in more than learning. Whether "sacked out" under the haystack or "shined-up" to the point of sleeping with the pigs, he remains an entertaining outrage, the newcomer who is the object of ridicule.

Polla, Per's wife, is a plump city girl from Fargo, North Dakota, who knows nothing about rural life. She thinks Fargo is the center of culture because of the many dishwashing machines, wireless radios, and sleeping porches there. Although the circumstances of their meeting are not given, Per brings Polla home from Fargo one spring when he had gone there

generelt gjennomgitt under påvirkning av eventyrserier som Phil Cranes *Wash Tubbs* (1924), George Storms *Phil Hardy* og *Bobby Thatcher* (1925—27) og Harold Grays *Little Orphan Annie* (1924) som alle koplet eksotiske eventyr sammen med hjemmestrikkede høyrevridde idéer.[7] *Han Ola og han Per* tar også opp tråden fra de første «morobøkene» som utkom som opptrykk av populære tegneserier. Fra 1921 ble Rosendahls tegneserier sendt ut i ialt åtte bøker. De ble brukt som en slags «lokkematpremie» for abonnentene på *Decorah-Posten*.

Familiepreget som kjennetegner de første årene av *Han Ola og han Per* er i tråd med den norsk-amerikanske immigrantlitteraturen og dens tradisjoner: å skildre immigrantens forhold til familien. Det viktigste for den norske immigranten var en bedre tilværelse, ikke bare for seg selv, men også for hele hans familie. Persongalleriet i Ola og Per-serien omfatter også en hel familie. De seks hovedpersonene er Ola, Per, Lars (Pers bror), Polla (Pers kone), Værmor (Pers svigermor) og Dada (barnet til Per og Polla). De fleste episodene handler om Ola og Per, men de andre personene er ofte med i handlingen, enten som støttespillere eller som motvekt til hovedpersonene. Olas kone Mari er med flere ganger, selv om hun som oftest er på vei til Minneapolis eller til Norge. Hver og en av disse skikkelsene er pussige, særlig fordi de alle er merket av selvmotsigelser og inkonsekvente trekk.

Med Ola og Per i sentrum skildrer serien disse to naboene som går gjennom en endeløs rekke av ulike erfaringer der den ene av dem alltid får en eller annen fantastisk idé. Per er antagelig hovedpersonen der han befinner seg midt blant familien sin. Han er fremstilt som den høye, langbente og skjeggete skikkelsen som alltid går med Derbyhatt og frakkeskjøter à la Prins Albert. Til tross for sitt distingverte utseende har han som oftest et eller annet verktøy i hånden. Per pønsker ustanselig ut nye idéer til patenter som gjør gården hans mer og mer avhengig av tekniske hjelpemidler. Dette er muligens en gjenspeiling av Rosendahls egen interesse for nye oppfinnelser, men sikkert er det iallfall at Ola og Per-serien har bidratt like mye til livet på landet som George Derby og Rube Goldbergs oppfinnelser bidro til bylivet. Patentene fører allikevel ikke til stort annet enn å gjøre daglig-livet mer innviklet, og bruken av dem ender i det rene kaos. Per har ikke særlig mer hell med seg som frier. Men etter at han vel er gift med Polla og er blitt far til Dada, påtar han seg rollen som familiens overhode med enerett til å ta alle avgjørelser, selv om disse ofte blir dyttet på ham av andre. Som autoritet både på

oppfinner- og familieområdet har Per *alazon*- eller skrytepave-rollen.

Ola er den snille naboen som gir gode og velmente råd, eller som søker hjelp hos «hr. Allviter» for alle problemene sine. Ola er *eiron*-skikkelsen som forblir rolig til en annen trenger råd, eller han selv trenger hjelp. Ola er alltid barhodet, han er kortvokst og iført overall, og er oftest å se med en høygaffel på skulderen. Noen av problemene hans skyldes trolig mangel på teknisk innsikt, eller manglende kjennskap til tekniske finesser. Allikevel ender rådslagningene med Per som oftest i kaos og forvirring, med Per som offer og Ola som den som ler sist, men best. Andre ganger er det Ola som er offer, eller begge to (23—25).

Den viktigste representanten for nykommeren til Amerika er Pers bror, Lars, som er «utdannet» både i Oslo og Berlin. Han er åpenbart en representant for den «lærde tosken». Hans første reaksjon når han kommer fra Norge er sjokk over det høye tempoet (20). Fra nå av kastes Lars fra det ene sjokket til det andre, og trekkes inn i de mest bisarre situasjoner som tenkes kan. Han får ofte oppgaver som han sier han mestrer til fullkommenhet, men etter som han setter i gang uten kjennskap til selve oppgavens art, ender det hele i total forvirring. Hans distingverte utseende, lange smale skjegg og frakk med flosshatt til, skjuler naivitet og manglende sunt folkevett. Når han ikke lenger klarer å hamle opp med bonde-Amerika, bestemmer «den lærde tosken» seg for å reise til Kina, fordi der, har han hørt, kan en mann ha flere koner. Men på veien skriver han til Per fra Hollywood og forteller at han har tatt jobb som misjonær der i stedet. Nå kan han benytte sin praksis i religiøs virksomhet til å hjelpe alle de «ugudelig flotte jentene» (101). Misjoneringen tar fort slutt, ettersom han stadig tørster etter «heimebrent». Lars, som sjelden er å se uten dunken sin, går i en stadig rus. Når han vender tilbake fra New York, hvor han angivelig har studert til kiropraktor, er det ikke bare lærdom han holder på å drukne i. Enten han ligger «slått ut» under høystakken eller sover ut rusen med grisene i grisebingen, er og blir han en evig skjensel og skam, nykommeren som gjør seg til latter.

Polla, Pers kone, er en lubben bypike fra Fargo, Nord-Dakota, som er helt ukjent med landlivet. Hun mener at Fargo er verdens sentrum på grunn av alle oppvaskmaskinene, radioene og soveverandaene. Selv om vi ikke får vite hvordan de møtte hverandre, fikk Per Polla med seg hjem fra Fargo da han en vår reiste dit i stedet for å pløye, slik naboen gjorde. Når han

instead of plowing as his neighbor had. One week later when he returns with his "pie fæs," his friend Ola is flabbergasted (91). But marriage between the city girl and the country boy is not always strawberries and cream. Speaking English more than the others, Polla misses the city and finds rural life difficult; Per's ineptness does not make him an ideal husband either. Every now and then they leave each other, but they cannot stand to be separated and then reunite.

Polla and Per's problems are not helped by the arrival of Værmor, Polla's mother from Fargo (21 November 1924). She not only represents the stereotyped mother-in-law, but she also is the hard-working pioneer woman. Tough, like Mammy Yokum in *Li'l Abner,* she finds no task too great, and nothing fazes her as far as work is concerned. Moreover, she cannot stand to see anyone loafing when there are farm chores to be done. But although she and Lars are unlike in their attitude toward work, they bear a startling resemblance in appearance. Neither is nature's prize. As Lars describes her, Værmor's "cheeks are pale . . ., her lips so red . . ., and her nose is like a rake handle" (250). Yet as soon as she arrives on the farm, she and Lars fall so in love that neither of them can work. After marriage, Lars still has his Lizzies of earlier days write to him. Once when he takes off for Canada to give lectures on birth control, he says, he has Værmor immediately on his neck. Through all their adventures, however, and even with Værmor's constant sniffing out the "moonshine," she and Lars always end up together. On one adventure when Værmor is carried off by a gorilla, she is rescued by none other than Lars (283).

Dada, the youngest of the characters and the only child of Per and Polla, completes the family. She shows her precocious inheritance as a baby for when she is left in the bureau drawer, she calls "Dada" (223). These amusing characters have become so familiar to many Norwegian-American families that they literally count Ola and Per as family members. They display enlarged drawings of them in living room photo galleries or even paint resemblances on kitchen match boxes.

Another aspect of the humor is the slapstick situation in which these unforgettable characters frequently find themselves. They are caught in a situation which can end in only one pattern — violence — but Norwegians miraculously survive. Somebody smashes the Ford, the mule smashes the person, or one character wallops another, but they come out of the catastrophe alive. There is no end to the ingenuity displayed in the creation of incidents. Per's gadgets shatter in bits and pieces; Ola's home remedies, such as washing hair in gasoline, bring disaster; and airplanes crash land, but there is never any bloodshed or fatal illness. Even when dynamite is used, and it often is, the situation explodes, but the characters involved are not hurt in the least, although they take a speedy space trip. The technique of exaggeration is used to blow up the situation to its wildest proportions yet still retain a relationship between the original situation and the exaggeration.

The literary artistry of *Han Ola og han Per* is evident not only in the characterization and situations but also in the imagery. The figures of speech, which are not overwhelming in number, are appropriately earthy and homely comparisons to farm life or the natural environment. Per gets wet as a herring (141), Lars sleeps like a pig (258) and looks like a pighouse (160), the rain comes down like a waterfall (314), and Værmor's brow is like snow drifts (234). Some of the verbal play includes puns on Lars' being "soaked" — with learning and liquor (171), Per's being saved by a bad "bumper" of the car (169), Per's being "finished" — but unable to function (131), the battle of "Bull Run" coming in a new edition (469), and Per's asking, after the bus has gone off the road, "Is this Decorah?" only to hear, "No, it's an accident" (230). Many proverbs are repeated in the titles, such as "The one who laughs last often laughs best" (44, 422, 443, 486), "Haste makes waste" (124), and "One should not believe everything one hears" (425).

From the standpoint of graphic artistry the cartoonist uses many of the usual comic conventions in a realistic, plain, rather crude style of drawing. The speech balloons are squared off in a box-like manner; hats rise from the heads to indicate surprise; sleep and snores are marked by the usual zzzzZZZZZ. One of the most interesting features is the close continuity of appearance and line from panel to panel and also from one strip to another. For example, when Lars loses part of his beard, the next series pictures him as partly beardless, but his beard slowly grows longer. When Værmor loses her hair, the next strips show her wearing a turban. The usual circles to indicate motions of characters are combined effectively with line continuity in many strips. Generally done in an understated style, the drawings nevertheless usually end with a climactic explosion of lines going in all directions. One of the most effective of all the drawings, however, is the depiction of back-seat driving (280) which after a confusion of circles and balloons ends in a blank.

Beyond the literary and graphic artistry, the historical value

en uke senere kommer tilbake med sin nye kone, blir vennen Ola målløs (91). Men ekteskapet mellom byjenta og bondegutten er ikke noen dans på roser. Polla, som snakker bedre engelsk enn de andre, savner byen og synes at livet på landsbygda er vanskelig. Pers klossethet gjør ham ikke til den perfekte ektemann heller. Nå og da skiller de lag, men orker ikke å leve alene, og kommer sammen igjen.

Polla og Pers problemer blir ikke mindre når Værmor kommer, Pollas mor fra Fargo (21. november 1924). Hun er ikke bare den stereotype svigermor, men også den arbeidssomme pionerkvinnen. Tøff som hun er, slik som Mammy Yokum i *Li'l Abner,* er ingen oppgave for hard for henne, og det skal mye til å vippe henne av pinnen når det gjelder arbeid og slit. Hun tåler ikke å se noen gå og slenge så lenge det er gårdsarbeid som skal gjøres. Men selv om hun og Lars er forskjellige i sine holdninger til arbeid, er de påfallende like av utseende. Ingen av dem er noen fryd for øyet. Ifølge Lars har Værmor «bleke kinn, røde lepper . . ., og nesen hennes ser ut som et riveskaft» (250). Allikevel blir hun og Lars forelsket i hverandre fra samme øyeblikk hun setter foten på gården, og det så ettertrykkelig at ingen av dem klarer å arbeide. Men selv etter at han har giftet seg, mottar Lars brev fra sine gamle venninner. Når han en gang reiser til Canada angivelig for å foreiese om fødselskontroll(!), får han Værmor på nakken øyeblikkelig. Men til tross for alle viderverdighetene, og selv om Værmor alltid kan lukte når han har smakt heimebrent, blir Værmor og Lars alltid forlikte til slutt. En gang Værmor blir bortført av en gorilla på en av ekspedisjonene deres, er det ingen mindre enn Lars som redder henne (283).

Dada, den yngste av skikkelsene og Per og Pollas eneste barn, er den siste i rekken. Allerede som baby røper hun hvor moden hun er når hun etterlates i kommodeskuffen og roper «Dada» (223).

Disse morsomme figurene er blitt så kjente og kjære for mange norsk-amerikanere at de faktisk betrakter Ola og Per som familiemedlemmer. De har forstørrede tegninger av dem hengende på veggen i spisestuen sammen med alle familiebildene, og de maler endog bilder av dem på fyrstikkeskene sine.

En annen side ved humoren er slapstick-situasjonene som de ofte havner i. De fanges opp i en situasjon som bare kan ende på en måte — i voldsomheter — men nordmenn har en egen evne til å overleve alt. Forden blir knust, en av figurene trampes ned av et muldyr, eller en av dem klabber til en annen, men alle slipper levende fra det. Oppfinnsomheten hos personene kjenner ingen grenser. Pers oppfinnelser knuses i tusen biter, Olas råd, som f.eks. å vaske håret i bensin, fører til katastrofe, fly kræsjer, men blodsutgydelser eller dødelige sykdommer forekommer aldri. Selv når dynamitt blir benyttet, og det hender, er det situasjonen, og ikke personene som eksploderer. Det eneste som skjer, er at de får seg en rask luftetur. Overdrivelsesteknikken brukes til å blåse opp situasjonen til de villeste proporsjoner, samtidig som forholdet mellom den opprinnelige situasjonen og overdrivelsen bevares.

De litterære egenskapene i *Han Ola og han Per* kommer fram ikke bare gjennom karakterskildring og situasjoner, men også gjennom billedbruken. Metaforene, selv om de ikke er så mange rent tallmessig, er treffende, med jordnære og hjemlige sammenligninger fra bondeliv eller miljøet: Per blir «våt som en sild» (141), Lars «sover som en gris» (258), og «ser ut som en svinesti» (160), det «regner som en foss» (314), og Værmors panne «er som en snøfonn» (234). Noen av ordlekene inneholder dobbeltbetydninger: Lars som drukner — i lærdom og brennevin (171), Per som reddes av støtfangeren (169), Per som er «ferdig», men ute av stand til å fungere (131), slaget ved Bull Run i ny utgave (469), og Per som spør, etter at bussen har kjørt av veien, «Er dette Decorah?», og får til svar, «Nei, det er bare en ulykke» (230). Mange ordtak blir benyttet i titlene, slik som «Den som ler sist, ler best» (44, 422, 443, 486), «Hastverk er lastverk» (124), og «Tro ikke alt du hører» (425).

Sett fra et grafisk utgangspunkt bruker tegneserieforfatteren mange av de vanlige komiske virkemidlene i en realistisk, enkel og ganske grovkornet stil. Snakkeboblene er delvis firkantede, hattene hever seg fra hodet som tegn på overraskelse, søvn og snorking betegnes på den vanlige måten med *zzzzzZZZZZ*. Et av de mest interessante trekkene er en gjennomført kontinuitet i utseende og linjer fra bilde til bilde. F. eks. når Lars mister litt av skjegget sitt, viser neste bilde ham delvis uten skjegg, og skjegget blir så gradvis lenger og lenger. Når Værmor mister håret, ses hun i neste bilde med turban på hodet. De vanlige rundingene som betegner at skikkelsene beveger seg, er virkningsfullt kombinert med helhet i alle linjer. Selv om tegningene stort sett er gjennomført i såkalt «understatement»-stil, ender de som regel i et klimaks av linjer som eksploderer i alle retninger. En av de mest virkningsfulle tegningene fremstiller den velkjente situasjon med bilpassasjeren som hele tiden blander seg inn i kjøringen (280). Etter et virvar av streker og rundinger i alle retninger, er den siste bilderammen helt tom.

Men serien har også sin historiske verdi ved siden av sin billed-

of the comic strip lies in its revelation of the way the Norwegian-American immigrant community thought and lived. Despite the comic distortions and the incongruities between the realism of the setting and characters and the fantastic actions and situations depicted, the humor vividly portrays common men and their daily lives. In the depiction of folklife several themes are developed: 1) the pains and tensions for the immigrant who wants to retain his ethnic identity at the same time that he is adjusting to American life with its constant changes; 2) the disruptive effect of gadgets and machines and the absurd pretentiousness of automated life; 3) the confusion of the human condition, or the world as nonsensical; and 4) the demonstration that the human being endures even though he is foolish, weak, and undignified.

The main humorous theme is certainly the tension between the dream and the real worlds of the immigrant. Throughout the seventeen-year life of the comic strip the characters never forget their Norwegian roots, nor do they give up their language in spite of their initial problems in social matters because they misunderstand American speech or signs. For example, when Per complains that he never has a chance with the young girls, Ola advises him that the problem is simply that he cannot speak "Yeinki." Following Ola's advice the next time he meets a young girl, he lifts his hat and greets her, "Hello, Pie Fæs." Per lands in the gutter where he comforts himself with the favorite sentimental song of Norwegians in America, "Kan du glemme gamle Norge?" ["Can You Forget Old Norway?"] (9). Initially baffled by the speed at which all the vehicles move in America, the newcomer Lars falls off on his first motorcycle ride (20). Soon after, he tries to keep up with cars, tractors, and airplanes and keep away from salesmen and sheriffs. But the adjustments made by the city girl who goes to the farm are just as difficult, as Polla discovers (102).

The educated newcomer experiences the most problems in coming to the farm, however. Struggling with new customs, Lars' attempt to put the crupper on Kate ends in his being kicked out of the barn (48). Nor can he drive the team, feed the calves, manage the mules, or cope with snakes. When he cooks soup, he uses meat from the skunk, and finally when he tries to spray poison on the potato bugs, he admits he prefers beautiful old Norway. "It is not easy to be a newcomer," he says (41). Even after Per and Ola are sure Lars is learning, he shows his ignorance of tilling the soil when he interprets the direction to follow the cow literally (500). When Lars finds his consolation in

"moonshine," he reveals his attachment for the old country by singing "Ja, vi elsker dette landet," the Norwegian national anthem (57), but often the effects of moonshine take him beyond chauvinistic consciousness (148). Eventually his ineptness leads only to a series of frustrated attempts at working not only as a farmer but also as a chiropractor, a missionary, a radio announcer, an artist, and a reducing specialist. His work efforts bring rags, not riches, so that finally his family threatens to put him in the poor house. Driven to near-madness by Værmor's domination, he ends up standing on top of the chimney and throwing bricks down on the people (487). His experiences bring him closer to insanity than success in a reversal of the "American Dream" theme which was also satirized by Sinclair Lewis, F. Scott Fitzgerald, and other critics.

Among the reasons for the immigrant's survival, however, are his willingness to attempt the impossible in spite of the odds and his insistence on retaining customs from the old country. In carrying out the impossible, Per and Ola each reveal themselves to be among the "natural born fools," such as Sut Lovingood created by George Washington Harris of the Southwestern humor tradition. The fools' actions bring punishment to themselves, and sometimes these foolish endowments help to reveal the hypocrisy of supposedly respectable members of society and then to punish them appropriately. When trying to control the cattle, Per's "natural born" characteristics get the better of him and he tries to stop the cattle from sneaking back into the barn and into another cow's stall. As often happens, the wrong object or person becomes the victim of a violent accident (13). Usually, however, the fool becomes the victim of his own "know-how," as when Per attempts to start the manure spreader (12). Only too often Per is laughed at by the people he tries to help, but sometimes they become the targets of ridicule. His most common means of coping with his world and realizing his dream is to come up with some complicated gadget. One example of this is his "sow force-feeder" which he plans to use so that the three pigs he will ship to market weigh 1500 pounds, thereby bringing him many thousand dollars. He is confident of his success because "it is a business which has never blown up, so to speak" until his pig explodes (16). Another invention of the mechanically inclined Per is his perpetual motor. This time the "educated fool" is helped by the practical Ola, who cranks the motor (266) so that the machine runs.

When members of mainstream society interfere with Per's, Ola's or Lars' likes, the Norwegians are not silent or inactive.

messige og kunstneriske kvalitet. Den skildrer det norsk-amerikanske immigrantsamfunnet, og hvordan menneskene her tenkte og levde. Til tross for alle komiske forvrengninger og uoverensstemmelsen mellom den realistiske miljøskildringen på den ene siden, og de fantastiske hendelsene skikkelsene i dette miljøet kommer ut for på den andre siden, gir humoren et levende bilde av alminnelige menneskers dagligliv. I folkelivsskildringen er flere temaer berørt: (1) smerten og spenningene den immigrant utsettes for som både vil beholde sin etniske identitet og samtidig tilpasse seg den urolige og skiftende amerikanske livsstilen, (2) den forvirring som patenter og oppfinnelser fører med seg, og de absurde pretensjoner som et liv fylt av maskiner skaper, (3) menneskets forvirrende tilværelse eller livet uten mening, og (4) den sannhet at mennesket overlever, selv om det er dumt, svakt og uverdig.

Det mest iøynefallende humoristiske tema er uten tvil spenningen mellom immigrantens drømmer og livet slik det virkelig er. I løpet av de sytten årene serien eksisterte glemte skikkelsene ikke et øyeblikk sine norske røtter. De gir ikke opp språket sitt selv når de til å begynne med får adskillige sosiale problemer fordi de stadig misforstår amerikansk tale eller skilter. Når Per f.eks. klager over at han aldri gjør lykke hos kvinner, sier Ola ham at det er fordi han ikke kan snakke «Yeinki». Neste gang Per møter en kvinne, husker han hva Ola har sagt, og hilser henne med ordene «Hallo, Pie Faes». Per lander hodestups i rennesteinen hvor han trøster seg med den sentimentale yndlingssangen til alle nordmenn i Amerika: «Kan du glemme gamle Norge?» (9). Lars som til å begynne med forvirres over alle de raske kjøretøyene i Amerika, faller av sykkelen på sin første tur på motorsykkel (20). Litt senere prøver han å holde følge med biler, traktorer og fly og å holde seg langt unna selgere og sheriffer. Men byjentas tilpasningsproblemer er like store, det får Polla erfare (102).

Den som får de største problemene når han kommer til gården, er allikevel Lars, den «velutdannede» nykommeren. Mens han er i ferd med å legge bakreimen på muldyret Kate i et forsøk på å venne seg til de nye skikkene, sparkes han ut av låven (48). Han kan heller ikke kjøre forspann, mate kalver, mestre muldyr eller overmanne slanger. Når han koker suppe bruker han skunkekjøtt, og når han prøver å sprøyte gift på potetbillene, innrømmer han at han savner vakre gamle Norge. «Det er ikke lett å være nykommer,» sier han (41). Selv etter at Per og Ola er sikre på at Lars er i ferd med å lære, røper han sitt manglende kjennskap til jordbruksarbeid når han misforstår instruk-

sene han får og tror at «følg kua» skal tolkes helt bokstavelig (500). Når Lars trøster seg med heimebrent, røper han sin tilknytning til gamlelandet og synger «Ja, vi elsker dette landet» (57), men andre ganger fører brennevinet til at han ikke har noen som helst form for nasjonal bevissthet, eller bevissthet i det hele tatt (148). Hans udugelighet fører ham til slutt opp i en mengde mislykte forsøk på de forskjelligste yrker, som kiropraktor, misjonær, hallomann i radio, kunstner, slankeekspert, foruten bonde. Men ingen av disse forsøkene bringer ham rikdom, snarere det motsatte, og til slutt truer familien med å sende ham på fattighuset. Værmor driver ham nesten til vanvidd, og til slutt ser vi ham på toppen av skorsteinen, der han står og kaster murstein på folk (487). Erfaringene hans bringer ham nærmere galskap enn suksess og er et vrengebilde av «Den amerikanske drømmen», som også Sinclair Lewis, F. Scott Fitzgerald og andre harselerte over.

Noen av årsakene til at immigrantene stort sett overlever, er at de er villige til å prøve det umulige, selv når de har alle odds mot seg, og at de stedig holder fast på skikkene fra gamlelandet. Ved å gjennomføre det umulige, viser Per og Ola seg som «de fødte idioter», slik som George Washington Harris' Sut Lovington — en skikkelse fra sørvesten. Fjolsenes handlinger fører til at de straffer seg selv, men av og til fører de samme tåpelighetene til at de såkalt respektable samfunnets støtter blir avslørt og får sin rette straff. Når Per skal gjete buskapen, er det hans medfødte instinkt som får ham til å hindre dyrene i å snike seg tilbake til låven, og inn i fjøset til en av de andre båsene. Som så ofte skjer, er det de gale personene eller tingene som blir utsatt for et eller annet voldsomt uhell (13). Men oftest er det tosken selv som blir offer for sin egen «allvitenhet», som når Per prøver å starte sin egen gjødselspreder (12). Per blir ofte ledd ut når han forsøker å hjelpe, selv om også andre kan bli utsatt for latteren. Det han som oftest tyr til når han strever med å klare seg, er en eller annen ny oppfinnelse. Et eksempel er «purketvangsforeren» som han har planer om å bruke når tre av purkene hans skal sendes på markedet. Hvis purkene veier 150 kilo hver, kan Per tjene flere tusen dollars. Han er sikker på å lykkes, «for det er jo en forretning som ikke har gått i lufta ennå, iallfall», helt til en av grisene virkelig *går* i lufta (16). En annen oppfinnelse som den maskingale Per er mester for, er en evighetsmotor. Denne gangen blir den lærde tosken hjulpet av praktiske Ola, som sveiver maskinen i gang (266).

De gangene medlemmer av samfunnet utenfor blander seg inn mot slike som Per, Ola eller Lars, er nordmennene hverken

The main victims of Per's dislike are book agents, unless they are girls (32). Also subject to ridicule are dentists (35), chiropractors (151), the sheriff (528), the local bureaucrats who administer farm relief (347, 348, 355, 367) and the politicians in Washington who passed a wife-exchange law which Lars took advantage of to exchange Værmor for a peanut roaster (578). The hard-working pioneer woman who ends up as boss in the house, as Værmor often does, is the target of much satire. The worst Værmor receives for spying to see if Lars has moonshine is a manure pie in her face (245), but other objects come her way as well. Actually there is always a type of justice meted out, as the immigrants disliked anyone who posed as high and mighty (44). There is a devastating attack on mankind in general when human beings are depicted as having non-human or animal qualities, especially when Per mistreats animals (194), and when Lars makes love to Værmor, praising her animal features at such length that he "falls in weakness and lies like a swine" (258), as he also does when he over-indulges in his jug. These attempts to expose that which was not what it seemed to be were further manifestations of the basic desire for regularity and congruity in life. Deviations from a rational, purposeful creation are ridiculed. The comic strips also suggest that in pioneer times people had to cope by many means — not the least of which were physical pranks, such as the upsetting of love-making by bringing in a cow (183). Any attacks on persons in authority reflected the basic attitude, but questionable logic, that "everybody is as good as everyone else — and a bit better."

Retaining ties with the folk culture and customs of Norway also contributes to the humorous situations of the immigrant. A typical Norwegian, Værmor must take time to have a little "kaffi-skvet," a wee drop of coffee, before she leaves the house even though the flood is coming with full force (390). On another occasion coffee revives Værmor when all other remedies fail (325), just as whiskey does for Lars (380). When Ola and Per are stranded in the North Dakota blizzard, whose skis do they find to save their lives but the ones they attribute to Per Hansa in Rølvaag's *Giants in the Earth* (451). When Lars downs rat poison, he shows the effect on him by vigorously dancing the Halling hat dance (416). Other evidences of Norwegian folk culture are found in telling numbskull stories (64), in blaming ghosts for the appearance of strange creatures (252, 369, 589), in recalling troll mischief (313, 341), and in singing traditional Norwegian songs, such as the national anthem, "Yes, We Love This Land of Ours" (57), the nostalgic "Can You Forget Old Norway?" (9), and "How Glorious is my Land of Birth" (49). The traditional habit of the Norwegian's finding the chief nourishment in "graut" or porridge is a theme of the strip from the first issues to the last (59, 175, 401, 556). If the porridge has not been made with cream from the cow that has just calved, the quality is inferior and not suitable, according to Ola's wife. Talking with his wife about her Ford, Ola quotes from Ibsen's *Peer Gynt*. "You can tell the big shots by their mounts," referring to Peer Gynt's riding into the Dovre mountains with the Greenclad Woman on a huge pig (8). Also ridiculed is the habit of joining fraternal organizations, such as the Sons of Norway, just for the sake of belonging to an "old outfit" of people from the Old Country. The best satire is on the currently popular search for ancestral roots, for when Ola and Per haul out the books to find out where the family stems from in Norway, Per points to the picture of grandpa — a gorilla (555).

Some of the best humor concerning the immigrant experience comes in a delightful parody of the adventure motive for immigration. The immigrants coming home from Siberia aboard the "*Spirit of Decorah*" land on an island where they undergo a series of fantastic encounters (274—354). After frightening meetings with snakes and gorillas, they decide to build their "castle in the sky" only to lay the foundation on stones which prove to be large turtles that wake up and walk away, wrecking the house. One of the first visitors to the island is Smart Aleck, an agent selling the "Sure Grip Automatic Monkey Wrench." When Per discovers the "artocarpus flapjackus" or pancake tree, he overeats to the point where he thinks he is dying, so he wills his hat to the Decorah Museum, the main Norwegian-American immigrant museum. After having difficulties in crossing a river, the immigrants are threatened by volcanic eruption, from which they take shelter in a bat-filled cave. After meeting a dinosaur, they tangle with a monkey who steals Lars' clothes. Værmor cries because Lars has to go naked, but he says that is nothing to get excited over. The New World Adam has an extra suit of clothes in the airplane. Eventually the group finds a home in a huge stove pipe, and then Værmor builds a raft to carry them back to civilization. But "things look dark for the pioneers." After several unsuccessful attempts to return to America, they finally arrive. They know they are home because Ola sees a vehicle marked "bus," but Per comments, "It says 'booze' on it so we are in the U.S.A." This delightful series of adventures ends with Ola and Per's appreciation speech upon

tause eller passive. Bokselgere er det verste Per vet, så sant de ikke er jenter (32). Tannleger (35), kiropraktorer (151), sheriffen (528), de lokale byråkatene som administrerer bondestønad (347, 348, 355, 367) og politikerne fra Washington som gjennomførte en konebyttelov som Lars brukte til å anskaffe en peanøtt-steker i bytte for Værmor — alle disse blir grundig gjort til latter. Den arbeidssomme pionerkvinnen som ender som sjefen i huset, blir også ofte latterliggjort. Det eneste Værmor oppnår når hun spionerer på Lars for å finne ut om han har heimebrent på seg, er en kukake midt i fjeset (245), og ting og gjenstander har i det hele tatt lett for å havne der hun befinner seg. Allikevel ender de fleste episodene med at rettferdigheten seirer, ettersom pionerene sterkt mislikte at noen mente de var bedre enn andre (44). Menneskeheten i sin helhet utsettes for heftige angrep når enkeltpersoner fremstilles som umenneskelige eller dyriske, f.eks. når Per vanskjøtter dyrene sine (194). Og når Lars gjør kur til Værmor og roser hennes ansiktstrekk i den mest groteske overdrivelse, ender han med å bli svak og «lyve som et svin» (258). Det samme skjer når han ligger under for sterke varer. Alle forsøk på å avsløre alt som ikke er slik det ser ut, røper et underliggende ønske om orden og regelmessighet i tilværelsen. Ethvert avvik fra fornuft og mening her i livet gjøres til latter. Tegneserien viser dessuten hvordan folk i pionertiden måtte klare seg som best de kunne, ikke minst ved rene skøyerstreker — som når elskovsstunden avbrytes av at kua kommer inn (183). Angrep på øvrighetspersoner er andre eksempler på grunnholdningen i serien, selv om den kanskje kan diskuteres: «enhver er like god som en annen, eller kanskje enda bedre».

Båndet med norsk folkekultur og norske skikker er også morsomme bidrag til immigrantenes situasjon. Værmor, som er typisk norsk, *må* ta seg tid til en liten «kaffiskvett» før hun forlater huset, selv om flommen står for døren (390). Ved andre anledninger er kaffe det eneste som får liv i henne når alle andre forsøk mislykkes (325), akkurat som med Lars og brennevin (380). Når Ola og Per går seg bort i snøstorm i Nord-Dakota, finner de skiene til ingen mindre enn Per Hansa, hovedpersonen i Ole Rølvaags *I de dage* (451). Når Lars svelger rottegift, klarer han hallingkastet som aldri før (416). Andre tegn på norsk folkekultur finnes i skrønene (64), troen på gjenferd som en forklaring på underlige skapninger (252, 369, 589), på overtro og trollskap (313, 341) og i de nasjonalromantiske sangene, fedrelandssangen «Ja, vi elsker» (57), den nostalgiske «Kan du glemme gamle Norge?» (9) og «Hvor herligt er mitt fødeland» (49). Nordmennenes tradisjonelle styrkemiddel — «graut» —

går igjen i serien fra begynnelse til slutt (59, 175, 401, 556). Hvis rømmegrøten ikke er kokt av fløte fra en ku som nyss har kalvet, er den lite tess, mener kona til Ola. Når Ola snakker med henne om Forden hennes, siterer han Ibsens Peer Gynt: «På kjøretøyet skal storfolk kjennes», som viser til scenen hvor Peer sammen med Den Grønnkledte rider inn i Dovre på en diger gris (8). Skikken å melde seg inn i brorskapsorganisasjoner, som f.eks. «Sønner av Norge» bare for å tilhøre gamlegarden fra landet der hjemme, blir også gjort til latter. Den beste satiren er på vår tids søken etter forfedrenes røtter, som når Per og Ola haler fram bøker for å finne ut hvor i Norge slekten stammer fra, og Per peker på bildet av bestefaren — en gorilla (555).

Et av de morsomste innslagene når det gjelder immigrantenes erfaringer finnes i en pussig parodi på «eventyrlysten» som det viktigste motiv for å utvandre. Immigrantene, som er på vei hjem fra en tur til Sibir i flyet «Ånden fra Decorah» lander på en øy hvor de kommer ut for de mest utrolige møter og sammentreff (274—354). Etter de skremmende møter med slanger og gorillaer bestemmer de seg for å bygge et «drømmeslott». Plutselig reiser grunnmuren seg og labber avgårde, og det viser seg at grunnsteinene ikke var annet enn kjempeskilpadder. En av de første som besøker øya er Smart Aleck, en agent som selger en «automatisk skiftenøkkel». Når Per oppdager «artocarpus flapjackus» eller pannekaketreet, forspiser han seg så kraftig at han tror han er døden nær. Han testamenterer hatten sin til Museet i Decorah, et sentrum for norsk-amerikansk immigranthistorie. Etter at immigrantene har strevd med å krysse en elv, trues de av vulkanutbrudd og søker ly i en hule full av flaggermus. De møter en dinosaurus og slåss med en ape som stjeler klærne til Lars. Værmor gråter fordi Lars må gå rundt naken, men han synes ikke det er noe å bli opphisset over: Denne Adam i Den Nye Verden har en reservedress liggende i flyet. Til slutt søker de tilflukt i en diger skorstein, og Værmor bygger så en flåte som kan ta dem tilbake til sivilisasjonen. Men «det ser mørkt ut for nybyggerne». Etter mange uhell kommer de endelig tilbake til Amerika. De er sikre på at de er hjemme, for Ola ser et kjøretøy som det står *bus* på, men Per bemerker: «Det står *booze* (brennevin) på den, så da er vi i USA.» Denne pussige eventyrserien ender med at Ola og Per begge priser seg lykkelige over å være tilbake i Amerika. Polla avbryter dem, hun har oppdaget en fant som ligger og sover under en høystakk — det er ingen annen enn Lars med dunken.

Immigrantenes viderverdigheter blir drevet gjøn med i andre ekspedisjoner også: en tur til Nordpolen hvor de finner Amund-

being back in America. This is interrupted by Polla's announcement that down by the haystack there is a sleeping tramp — Lars with his jug.

The adventures of immigrants are mocked frequently in other trips: a North Pole trip where the immigrants find Amundsen's plane and Andrée's balloon (196—216); a trip to North Dakota during which, after being buried by a blizzard, they set up a shopping center with Per and Ola's runabout 5 and 10 cents store, Polla's lunch counter, Værmor's "bjuti" shop, and Dr. Lars' "redoosing" specialist's salon (446—476); and an attempted visit to the Chicago World's Fair (511—539) which ends with a robbery that eventually brings Ola and Per a large monetary reward for their return of the gold. These Gilligan's Island adventure series are not only directly related to immigration humor but they parallel the changes noted in comic strips of the late 1920's and 1930's from family funnies to adventure series.[8]

The other themes, already mentioned briefly in the main theme of immigrant adjustment, are developed quite extensively throughout the comic strip. Per's perpetual invention of a complex mechanism that wears itself out and everyone connected with trying to make it work appears throughout the entire series. Whenever Per encounters a little commonplace problem whether in the house, the barn, or the field, he attempts to "solve" it by inventing a fanciful machine. For the house he created the dirty clothes chute (109), a dishwashing machine (106), a hoist for bringing dishes to the table (410), a Hoover Commission kitchen-floor cleaning device (413), a gimmick for emptying the dish water (505), the "lazy man's jump bed" (409) and an electric comb (506). Of course, part of the irony of the humor is that many of these gimmicks anticipated real technological developments.

The endless contraptions for the farm work included a knock-out grub machine (122), a staple puller (237), a weather balloon (256), an electric fan to drive the windmill (270), an egg-cleaning machine (272), a wood-cutting machine (361), an electric pig fence (377), an air-pull cultivator (384), a cyclone chicken house cleaner (408), a self-cleaning cow barn (476), a rotary hog feeder (502), an air-push hog loader (503), a haystack loader (518), a whirl-wind steam chopper (540), a Model 34 Farm Bjuro [dresser] operated by compressed air (557), an iron cow (387), a tip-over, quick-oiling windmill (558), a high-speed manure spreader (567) and even a shock-absorbing wall (425). A lightning postpuller (554) illustrates how these inventions symbolized man's ability to expend maximum effort to create a machine to achieve what can be done more simply by hand, for Per and Ola spend more time getting the gadget in working order than Lars does in completing the task with the spade (554). But with the machine the person becomes a working part, usually the one who botches the mechanism. These inventions remind us that the automated life is not everything it is supposed to be. Far more rigid than man, the contraptions suggest that human values can survive in the New World only as long as man is flexible and able to laugh at his own creations. As Walter Winchell quipped about Rube Goldberg's works, "Generations of Americans have roared with laughter at Rube Goldberg's machines — but the combined scientists of the world cannot — and never will — produce a machine which laughs at a man."[9] For this, Rosendahl's Brave New World offered no possibilities either.

The Norwegian's gadgets were used to control people, too, such as the device to get rid of book agents (153), the safety pedestrian catcher (499), and the gimmick Lars used to seed from an airplane (378). The changing world of machines is also evident in the vehicles — from the motorcycle to the Ford, to the airplane, and finally to a "new grasshopper" that looks like the helicopter. Other inventions which the immigrants learn to use are the telephone, the wireless, and the Victrola. The basic point behind all of these strips seems to be that in spite of technological advances human beings never really change. Although man may expand his control of his environment or enlarge its sphere by coming to a new land, he does not change radically either his character or the meaning of life. But life changes, and people have to adjust — or be destroyed by violence. Progress is really an illusion. We human beings delude ourselves into "thinking that we're pushing ahead, but when we stop we're at the start."[10]

But if human beings don't change, the one certain result of their simply being alive is confusion. Much of the humor of the immigrants is the result of the characters' merely trying to adjust to the inevitable changes of daily life brought on because people choose different clothes styles, need cures for disease or weakness, fall in love and marry, struggle with daily tasks, and even spend a few hours in recreation. In *Han Ola og han Per,* Værmor throws away her out-dated knickers; Lars' clothes shred into rags; Værmor tries Dr. Lars' home hair treatments (262—263); Værmor and Lars find their courting interrupted by bees, wasps, and cows (228); Per and Ola use nitroglycerin to

sens fly og Andrées ballong (196—216), en tur til Nord-Dakota hvor de etter et voldsomt uvær setter opp butikk med Per og Olas mobile billigsjappe, Pollas lunsjdisk, Værmors «bjuti»-butikk og Dr. Lars' «slankeinstitutt» (446—476). De forsøker også å besøke Verdensutstillingen i Chicago (511—539), men kommer i stedet opp i et ran. Ola og Per får en stor pengebelønning fordi de finner og leverer det stjålne gullet tilbake. Disse eventyrreisene i «Gilligan Island»-stilen er ikke bare immigranthumor, men gjenspeiler den utviklingen som finner sted i alle tegneserier, både familie- og eventyrserier, fra slutten av 1920- og 1930-årene.[8]

De andre temaene, som såvidt er nevnt allerede i forbindelse med grunntemaet, immigrantenes tilpasningsproblemer, utvikles videre gjennom hele serien. Pers evinnelige oppfinnelser av innviklede maskiner som ødelegger seg selv og alle som forsøker å bruke dem, går igjen i hele serien. Hver gang Per støter på et problem, selv det aller minste, prøver han å «løse» det ved å finne opp en eller annen fantastisk maskin. Inne i huset har han funnet opp «skittentøykasteren» (109), en oppvaskmaskin (106), en heiseinnretning som bringer serviset fram til matbordet (410), en tingest som tømmer ut oppvaskvannet (505), «dovenpeisens fjærseng» (409), og en elektrisk kam (506). Noe av det ironiske ved flere av disse oppfinnelsene, er at de faktisk varsler oppfinnelser som senere virkelig kom.

Blant de evinnelige tingestene til bruk i gårdsarbeidet er en stubbebryter (122), en stolpeoppdrager (237), en værballong (256), en elektrisk vifte til å drive vindmøllen med (270), en eggeskrellermaskin (272), en vedhoggermaskin (361), et elektrisk grisegjerde (377), en trykkluftplog (384), en «virvelvind-hønsehus-vasker» (408), en selvrensende låve (476), en roterende grisemater (502), en luftdrevet griselaster (503), en høystakklaster (518), en «virvelvind-damphogger» (540), en Farmbyrå (kommode) Modell 34 som drives med kompressorluft (557), ei jernku (387), en selvsmørende, nedfellbar vindmølle (558), en hurtiggående gjødselspreder (567) og til og med en støtsikker vegg (425). Disse oppfinnelsene viser menneskets tilbøyelighet til å bruke tid og krefter på å skape maskiner til å utføre operasjoner som lettest lar seg gjøre ved håndkraft. Per og Ola bruker nemlig mer tid på å få patentene til å virke enn Lars gjør på å bli ferdig bare ved hjelp av en spade (554). Ved å bruke maskinene blir mennesket selv en del av maskineriet, som oftest den delen som forstyrrer maskinen. Disse oppfinnelsene minner oss om at det mekaniserte liv ikke er blitt hva man håpet på. Alle tingestene som er mindre fleksible enn mennesket

antyder at menneskeverdier bare kan overleve så lenge menneskene er i stand til å le av seg selv. Som Walter Winchell så treffende bemerket om Rube Goldbergs verk: «Generasjoner av amerikanere har brølt av latter over Rube Goldbergs maskiner — men alle verdens vitenskapsmenn kan ikke produsere en maskin som ler av menneskene».[9] Heller ikke Rosendahls «vidunderlige nye verden» ga muligheter for dette.

Nordmennenes oppfinnelser skulle også brukes til å kontrollere menneskene — som f.eks. metoden for å bli kvitt bokselgere (153), «sikkerhetsoppfangeren» av fotgjengere (499), og patenten som Lars brukte da han skulle så åkeren fra et fly (378). Maskinenes omskiftelige verden vises tydelig gjennom kjøretøyene også, fra motorsykkelen til Forden til flyet, og endelig til den «nye gresshopperen» som ser ut som et helikopter. Andre oppfinnelser som immigrantene lærer seg å benytte er telefonen, den «trådløse» radioen og Victrolaen. Det grunnleggende prinsipp bak alt dette er at mennesket aldri forandrer seg til tross for alle teknologiske fremskritt. Selv om mennesket kan utvide kontrollen over sine omgivelser, eller sine grenser ved å reise til et annet land, forandres ingenting radikalt, verken når det gjelder dets egen personlighet eller selve meningen med livet. Livet derimot forandrer seg, og vi må tilpasse oss — eller gå til grunne i voldsomheter. Fremskritt er egentlig en illusjon. Vi mennesker narrer oss selv når vi tror at vi stadig går videre, for «når vi stopper er vi tilbake ved utgangspunktet».[10]

Men selv om mennesket ikke forandres, så er forvirring det eneste som er sikkert her i livet. En stor del av humoren ligger i skikkelsenes forsøk på å tilpasse seg de uunngåelige forandringer som finner sted i dagliglivet, bare fordi folk velger ulike klesmoter, trenger kur for sykdom eller svakheter, forelsker og gifter seg, eller til og med bruker noen timer til ren avslapning. I *Han Ola og han Per* kasserer Værmor de gamle nikkersene sine, Lars' klær blir til filler, Værmor prøver Dr. Lars' hjemmepermanent (262—263), Værmor og Lars får sine elskovsstunder avbrutt av bier, hveps og kuer (228), Per og Ola bruker nitroglyserin til å blåse skinnet av ovnsstekte poteter (107), og hele gruppen overlever såvidt å spille dam og høre på radioen (140, 260). Ofte eksploderer disse hendelsene i voldsomheter, av og til ved hjelp av dynamitt. Uhellene og viderverdighetene dramatiserer menneskets begrensninger og bærer bud om at kaos er vår egentlige, grunnleggende situasjon.

Slutt-temaet er altså menneskets komiske forsøk på å bygge bro mellom to verdener: rent geografisk Den Gamle og Den Nye Verden, og teknologisk ved å stille det mekaniske og innviklede

blow the skins off baked potatoes (107); and the whole group barely survives playing checkers and listening to the radio (140, 260). Often these simple activities explode into fiery violence, sometimes caused by the use of dynamite. These fumbles and falls dramatize the limitations of all human beings and suggest that chaos is the basic human situation.

The final theme then is that in the humorous struggles of the human being as he bridges two worlds — both the geographical one of the Old and New Worlds and the technological one of the mechanically complicated versus the simple — the individual endures. Certainly Ola and Per grow to mythic proportions, for despite their hardships and catastrophes, they end their existence by going off on a trip to Norway. They take in stride the daily frustrations and problems, and despite constant disaster, they continue to work to improve their lot. Væermor, too, is put to the greatest test not only by her family but also by social enemies, yet she wins by foiling robbers and even helping Lars to regain his self-direction. Lars is the one who comes closest to succumbing to the insanity of life in the New World, yet in the last strip he is running to catch the plane.

The humor of Rosendahl's *Han Ola og han Per* is valuable for history and literary art. As history it depicts the tension between the immigrant's vision of the Promised Land and his actual encounters with the New World with its increasing reliance on technology to complicate even the most simple human process. As literature it offers vivid characters who survive the chaos of everyday living as well as the violence of fantastic adventures. Best of all, Rosendahl's comic strip offers these riches with amusement. *Han Ola og han Per* deserves a special place not only in Norwegian-American immigrant culture but in American and Norwegian culture at large.

NOTES

1 *Han Ola og han Per* is currently reprinted in *The Western Viking,* published in Seattle, Washington, and in several Minnesota newspapers such as *The Valley Journal* and *The Starbuck Times.*
2 Each of the 599 comic strips of *Han Ola og han Per* is identified by parenthetical reference to the number of the comic strip in the "Order of Publication." This list of comic strips arranges them by date of issue in the *Decorah-Posten,* but adds the Rosendahl number (for Nos. 1—511), the volume number of the collected edition in which the comic strip was reprinted by Anundsen Publishing Co., Decorah, Iowa, and the page of the strip which was assigned by numbering consecutively within the volume.
3 Odd S. Lovoll, "*Decorah-Posten*: The Story of an Immigrant Newspaper," in *Norwegian-American Studies and Records,* 27 (1977), 77 and 96.
4 *N. W. Ayer & Son's American Newspaper Annual and Directory* (Philadelphia, 1920), p. 291; 1935, p. 287; 1950, p. 323; and 1972, p. 343. The circulation of *Decorah-Posten* numbered 29,545 in 1935 and 5,867 in 1972.
5 Interview, Frederick Rosendahl, Minneapolis, Minnesota, June 10, 1981.
6 *Decorah-Posten,* 8 January 1926, p. 5. Printed in translation p. 5.
7 Jerry Robinson, *The Comics: An Illustrated History of Comic Strip Art* (New York: Berkley Publishing Corporation, 1976), pp. 57, 71, 88.
8 Stephen Becker, *Comic Art in America* (New York: Simon and Schuster, 1959), p. 86.
9 Peter C. Marzio, *Rube Goldberg: His Life and Work* (New York: Harper and Row Publishers, 1973), p. 197.
10 Marzio, p. 175.

opp mot det enkle. Og mennesket overlever begge. Ola og Per får mytiske proporsjoner, for på tross av slit og ulykker ender de sitt «liv» med å reise hjem til Norge. De har sin rikelige del av daglige skuffelser og problemer, men til tross for stadige uhell fortsetter de med å prøve å forbedre tilværelsen. Værmor settes også på de største prøvelser, ikke bare av sin familie, men også av omverdenen. Allikevel seirer hun — hun griper tyver, og hun fører selv Lars inn på nye veier. Lars er den som kommer ulykken nærmest, fordi han nesten går til grunne i Den Nye Verdens galskap. Men i den siste episoden løper han for å rekke flyet.

Rosendahls humor slik den kommer til uttrykk i *Han Ola og han Per* har både historisk og litterær verdi. Som historie gir den oss et bilde av spenningen mellom immigrantens drøm om Det forjettede land og hans faktiske møte med Den Nye Verden og dens økende avhengighet av teknologien — som problematiserer ethvert menneskelig gjøremål, selv det aller enkleste. Litterært gir den oss livaktige skikkelser som overlever hverdagslivets kaos såvel som de mest fantastiske eventyr. Men det beste av alt er at Rosendahl gir oss disse rikdommene med humor. Derfor fortjener *Han Ola og han Per* sin plass i amerikansk og norsk kultur som helhet, og ikke bare innen den norsk-amerikanske immigrantkulturen.

NOTER

1 Merk at denne innledningen tar opp til diskusjon hele Rosendahls serie med sine 599 episoder og ikke bare de 223 som her er gjengitt. Se den komplette listen med datoer bakerst i boken. *Han Ola og han Per* trykkes for tiden opp i *The Western Viking,* som utgis i Seattle, og i flere Minnesota-aviser som f.eks. *The Valley Journal* og *The Starbuck Times.*

2 Hver enkelt av de 599 episodene av *Han Ola og han Per* identifiseres ved hjelp av et nummer i parentes, som tilsvarer det nummer denne episoden har i listen sist i boken. Episodene er ordnet etter utgivelsesdato i *Decorah-Posten.* I tillegg kommer Rosendahls egen nummerering (no. 1—511) og henvisning til det bind hvor de samlede utgaver av tegneserien befinner seg (Anundsen Publishing Co., Decorah, Iowa ga serien ut), samt til det sidetall hver enkelt episode har fått tildelt innen hvert bind.

3 Odd S. Lovoll, «*Decorah-posten*: The Story of an Immigrant Newspaper» i *Norwegian-American Studies and Records,* 27 (1977), 77 og 96.

4 *N. W. Ayer & Son's American Newspaper Annual and Directory* (Philadelphia, 1920), s. 291: 1935, s. 287: 1950, s. 323: og 1972, s. 343. Opplagstallet for *Decorah-Posten* var på 29,545 i 1935 og 5,867 i 1972.

5 Intervju, Frederick Rosendahl, Minneapolis, Minnesota, 10. juni, 1981.

6 *Decorah-Posten*, 8. januar 1926, s. 5. Diktet er trykt i sin helhet s. 5.

7 Jerry Robinson, *The Comics: An Illustrated History of Comic Strip Art* (New York: Berkley Publishing Corporation, 1976), ss. 57, 71, 88.

8 Stephen Becker, *Comic Art in America* (New York: Simon and Schuster, 1959), s. 86.

9 Peter C. Marzio, *Rube Goldberg: His Life and Work* (New York: Harper and Row Publishers, 1973), s. 197.

10 Marzio, s. 175.

The Language of *Han Ola og han Per*

Einar Haugen

1

Much of the humor that captivated the readers of *Decorah-Posten* when they chuckled over Rosendahl's comic strip was due to the speech of the characters. In the following essay I shall try to explain why this was so, hopefully in a non-technical way so that readers who are not familiar with Norwegian may also appreciate it. When one translates, the humor of dialect is inevitably lost, and it is not possible merely to substitute an American dialect for the Norwegian. Conditions in the two countries are just too different. American writers have exploited dialects for humorous purposes, for example James Russell Lowell in writing about his New Englanders, or Joel Chandler Harris in depicting his southerners.[1] Comic characters have also appeared in dialect guise, as Snuffy Smith with his hillbilly speech or the Katzenjammer Kids with a kind of American German dialect.[2]

While these dialects each had its merits and its purpose, none of them approaches the authenticity and subtlety of Rosendahl's gallery of characters. He drew on his personal observation of the large and complex Norwegian immigrant community that was his birthplace and his lifetime home. The small town of Spring Grove was the center of a settlement founded in the 1850's in the southeastern corner of Minnesota. According to its historian, O. S. Johnson, there were about 20,000 Norwegians in 1920 in an area some twenty by thirty miles in extent.[3] Not far away, across the Iowa border, there was an equally impressive area, with Decorah as its center, the home not only of the newspaper with nationwide circulation, *Decorah-Posten*, publisher of Rosendahl's strip,[4] but also of the first and for a long time most prestigious Norwegian-American institution of higher learning, Luther College.[5]

2

The characters of Rosendahl's strip are individualized by their speech to a degree that would do credit to a novelist. It is not easy to write dialogue characterizing various persons in ways that are both authentic and readable. If it gets too authentic, so that it would meet the demands of a scientific linguist, it becomes unreadable. If it is to be readable, it must not be too unlike what its readers are accustomed to see. Speakers of dialect often have a harder time reading their own speech when it is written than the standardized language of the land. Rosendahl worked out a compromise that gave him two dimensions of identification. One was the speaker's Norwegian dialect, which reflected his and his wife's background. The other was the degree of English usage, which placed the speaker on a Norwegian-English spectrum, ranging from the newcomer who can't speak "yeinki" to the uppity city girls who speak nothing but English. While the Norwegian dialects identified the speaker's place of origin and social position, the continuum from pure Norwegian to pure English reflected his or her American experiences, their "acculturation," to use a fancy word that they would not have understood.[6]

The spoken forms of Norwegian must be seen against a background of the language of writing, which the immigrants brought with them from Norway. In our comic strip this is best represented by the captions, which may have been furnished by the editors, and in any case generally agreed with the style and spelling of the rest of the paper. This was characterized by having Gothic type, capital letters on the nouns, and a spelling that differed very little from that of Danish. We may call it "Dano-Norwegian," as we might call the language of the United States "Anglo-American," to mark that there are or were some minor differences. The Danish orthography was a legacy of over four centuries of domination by Denmark, to which Norway had been subjected from 1380 to 1814.[7]

By 1918 a century of agitation and reform had greatly altered the language situation in Norway. Reforms of 1907 and 1917 had replaced the Danish spelling with a Norwegian one; these would be followed in 1938 by an even more radical popularization of the language. The result has been to make contemporary Norwegians find the style of *Decorah-Posten* of that day almost intolerably and comically old-fashioned. Examples from the early captions here are *fik*, now *fikk* 'got'; *paa,* now *på* 'on'; *Frierfærd,* now *frierferd* 'courting'; *optræder,* now *opptrer* 'appears, functions'; *Modtagelse,* now *mottakelse* 'reception'. But these and other reforms, which we need not pursue further here, found little response among the emigrants. To them the language they had learned to read in school, whether in Norway or in America, was sanctified by being the language of their catechism, their Bible, their books, and their press.[8] Even though the reforms tended to bring Norwegian closer to their own speech, the emigrants had a vested interest in the written language which made the owners of their newspapers unwilling to risk losing them as subscribers.

Rosendahl was of course familiar with these newer tendencies in Norwegian language development, since papers like *Decorah-Posten* often carried news stories about the heated language controversies back home. But there is no evidence in

1

Mye av den humoren som fengslet leserne av *Decorah-Posten* da de humret over Rosendahls tegneserie kan tilskrives språket personene brukte. Dette essay er et forsøk på å forklare hvorfor dette var tilfelle. Jeg skal forsøke å gjøre det på en slik måte at lesere som ikke kan norsk også vil ha glede av det. Det er ikke til å unngå at dialekthumor blir borte når man oversetter, og det er ikke mulig å løse det problemet ved å erstatte den norske dialekten med en amerikansk. Forholdene i de to landene er *for* forskjellige. Amerikanske forfattere har brukt dialekt for å oppnå komisk virkning, som f.eks. James Russell Lowell gjør når han skriver om sine skikkelser fra New England, eller Joel Chandler Harris når han beskriver sine sørstatspersoner.[1] Komiske skikkelser har også forekommet i dialektforkledning, som Snuffy Smith med sitt «Hillbilly» språk eller Katzenjammer barna som snakker en slags amerikansk-tysk dialekt.[2]

Disse dialektene hadde sin verdi og sin hensikt, men ingen av dem kan sammenlignes med Rosendahls persongalleri når det gjelder ekthet og nyanserikdom. Han benyttet sine kunnskaper om det store og mangfoldige norske immigrantsamfunnet der han ble født og der han bodde hele sitt liv. Den lille byen Spring Grove var sentrum for en koloni som ble grunnlagt i 1850-årene i det sørøstlige hjørnet av Minnesota. Lokalhistorikeren O. S. Johnson har berettet at ca 20.000 nordmenn bodde der i 1920 i et område som var ca. 32 × 48 km stort.[3] Ikke så langt unna, over grensen til Iowa, var et annet område som også var av stor betydning. Decorah var sentrum i dette område. Her ble *Decorah-Posten* med Rosendahls tegneserie utgitt, en avis som ble lest over hele Amerika.[4] Her var også Luther College,[5] det første og lenge det mest velrenommerte norsk-amerikanske lærested for høyere utdannelse.

2

Personene i Rosendahls tegneserie karakteriseres individuelt ved språket de snakker, til en grad som en forfatter ville hatt all ære av. Det er ikke lett å skrive dialoger som karakteriserer forskjellige personer slik at de både blir autentiske og leseverdige. Blir dialekten for vitenskapelig, blir den uleselig. Hvis den skal være leselig må den ikke skille seg for mye ut fra det leserne er vant til å se. Det er ofte vanskeligere for folk som snakker dialekt å lese sin egen dialekt på trykk enn å lese landets offisielle språk. Rosendahl utarbeidet et kompromiss som gav ham et dobbelt sett av identiteter. Det ene var personens norske dialekt som avspeilet hans egen og konens norske bakgrunn. Det andre

representerte bruken av engelsk som plasserte personen på en norsk/engelsk skala, fra nykommeren som ikke kan snakke «yeinki» til de viktige bypikene som bare snakker engelsk. Mens de norske dialektene markerte talernes sosiale posisjon og geografiske opprinnelse, representerte overgangen fra rent norsk til rent engelsk deres amerikanske erfaringer og deres tilpasning til et nytt kulturmønster.[6] De norske dialektene må sees mot bakgrunn av det skriftspråket innvandrerne bragte med seg fra Norge. I våre tegneserier er dette best representert ved overskriftene. Disse ble muligens forfattet av avisens redaktør. Det var i alle fall overensstemmelse mellom overskriftene og avisens stil og rettskrivning forøvrig. Karakteristiske trekk var gotisk skrift, store forbokstaver på substantivene, og en rettskrivning som skilte seg lite fra dansk. Vi kan kalle den dansk-norsk, liksom vi kan kalle språket i Amerika «anglo-amerikansk» for å markere at det er, eller var, forskjellig fra britisk engelsk. Den danske ortografien var en arv fra mer enn fire århundrer dansk herredømme (1380—1814).[7]

Et århundre med agitasjon og reform hadde medført store forandringer i språksituasjonen innen 1918. Ved rettskrivningsreformene i 1907 og 1917 hadde norske stavemåter erstattet de danske. I 1938 ble det foretatt ytterligere radikale forandringer i språket. Resultatet er blitt at vår tids nordmenn finner stilen i *Decorah-Posten* både komisk og håpløst gammeldags. Eksempler fra overskriftene er *fik* for *fikk; paa* for *på; Frierfærd* for *frierferd; optræder* for *opptrer; Modtagelse* for *mottakelse*. Disse og andre reformer, som vi ikke behøver å gå nærmere inn på her, fant liten respons blant immigrantene. Det språket de hadde lært å lese på skolen var hellig for dem, enten de hadde lært det i Norge eller i Amerika: det var språket i katekismen, i Bibelen, i bøkene og avisene deres.[8] Selv om reformene hadde ført norsk nærmere talespråket hadde emigrantene fra før 1907 en fast forankring i det gamle skriftspråket, noe som gjorde at eierne av avisene nødig ville risikere å miste dem som abonnenter.

Rosendahl kjente selvfølgelig til de nye tendensene i norsk språkutvikling, da aviser som *Decorah-Posten* ofte bragte artikler om den hissige debatten omkring språksituasjonen hjemme. Men det er ingen ting i tegneseriene som tyder på at disse hadde noen virkning på hans dialoger. Ortografien i overskriftene var fortsatt dansk-norsk fra før 1907. Dialektord og amerikanismer ble gjengitt i anførselstegn, som f.eks. «karsen» (bilen, 1), «fixer» (steller, 5), «borde teacher'n» (ha læreren i pensjon, 11).

his cartoons that they had any effect on his dialogue. The captions continued to be written in Dano-Norwegian orthography from before 1907, marking dialect words and Americanisms with quotation marks, as in the examples "karsen" the car (1), "fixer" fixes (5), "borde teacher'n" board the teacher (11).

Against this background of a stiff and rather conservative Dano-Norwegian, associated only with the written word, it is therefore impressive that Rosendahl boldly struck out on the uncharted seas of daily speech. Some of his spellings still show the influence of writing, but most of them are so closely akin to immigrant speech that it must have created a hilarious feeling of emotional release. Here the emigrants could recognize themselves, or perhaps rather their neighbors. "This," they could say, "is not the preacher's and the schoolteacher's language! This is our kind of talk, just as funny and homely as we ourselves." The solemn gave way to the slapstick.

3

Ola and Per are marked as non-standard, i.e. rural dialect speakers, from the outset. The very way in which their names are presented, as "Han Ola" and "Han Per," is a virtually universal form of Norwegian rural speech: a proper noun required that an article of the appropriate sex precede it: *han* 'he' for males, *ho* or *hu* 'she' for females. Outlawed in standard writing and in cultivated urban speech, it gives a cozy feeling to the names. Silent letters are dropped in the spelling, sometimes without making any real difference in the pronunciation, as when Rosendahl writes *de* for *det* 'it' or *huse* for *huset* 'the house'. This kind of thing has been called "eye dialect," since it is only for the eye, as when English writers replace *though* with *tho* or *clothes* with *clo'es*. But their speech also marks forms that are truly characteristic of folk speech, e.g. with diphthongs like *ei* for *e* in *veit* 'know' *(vet/ved), au* for *ø* in *skaut* 'shot' *(skjøt-/skjød),* and *øi* (now *øy*) in *øi* 'island' *(ø)* or *høire* 'hear' *(høre).* In Norway the diphthongal forms were being adopted or encouraged in official spelling reforms, but among the emigrants they were still strange and amusing. We might compare it to the consistent use by a Supreme Court justice of forms like "ain't" or "he don't."

But Rosendahl has done more than place his characters solidly among the rural folk to which most of them belonged, in Norway as in America. He gave each of them a special identity by providing them with different folk dialects. The skill and

consistency with which he did this shows that he must himself have been bidialectal in Norwegian, besides knowing well the forms of written and spoken standard.

There is a very marked distinction in speech in Norway between what we may call the Midland mountain valleys and the eastern Lowlands. As we recreate from the spelling the spoken forms used by Ola and Per, we discover that they consistently make distinctions that place them on different sides of the line that runs between the central highlands and the eastern lowlands. Ola is the mountain man, whom we may call the "highlander," Per is the "lowlander," to parallel a similar distinction from Scotland. For 'I' Ola says *e,* Per *je;* 'she' is *ho* vs. *hu;* 'her' (unstressed) is *'o* vs. *'a;* 'we' is *me* vs. *vi;* 'they' is *dei* vs. *dom.* Besides these differences in the pronouns we find some of the more common adverbs: 'not' is *intje* (soon changed to *inkje*) vs. *itte;* 'how' is *køs* vs. *haas;* 'what' is *ko* or *kø* vs. *haa,* etc. In each case the "highland" form is more different from the urban forms, and more like Old Norse (or the New Norse created by Aasen in the 1850's on the basis of the more conservative dialects).

The differences are sometimes directly juxtaposed in one conversation. In strip 5 Per is telling Ola to "hang on to her tail": *Holdt i rompa paa 'a,* and Ola agrees: *E skal' nok hald 'o i rova e* "I'll hang on to her tail." Here 'hold' is *holdt* vs. *hald,* 'tail' is *rompa* vs. *rova,* the pronoun is *'a* vs. *'o.* One of the shibboleths of Norwegian dialects is the feminine definite article, whether it should be written *-i* or *-a:* Ola often uses *-i,* Per always *-a,* cf. *höndi* 'the hand' (30), *øksi* 'the axe' (10), *fili* 'the field' (11) vs. *eika* 'the oak' (2), *møkka* 'the manure' (32). Ola has a particularly striking form for some of his articles in the plural: *føtadn* 'the feet' *grisidn* 'the pigs', where Per would use *-an* or even *-a: tankan* 'the thoughts' (25), *kalva* 'the calves' (40). Ola occasionally uses a verb plural: *sko* 'shall' (7), *leva* 'live' (12), Per never. Ola has a vowel change in the present of strong verbs, e.g. *fær* 'gets' (19, 26), *slær* 'strikes' (35), which Per lacks, e.g. *faar* (25, 32). These examples will do; one could multiply them indefinitely.

In one cartoon Ola and Per tell us that subscribers to the paper have asked just where they come from. They pretend to look in reference books and encyclopedias, only to find that their grandfathers are gorillas. This spoof on the theory of evolution does not mean that Rosendahl was ignorant of the origins of his characters. On the contrary, it is evident not only from the forms themselves, but from our knowledge of his community

Med dette som bakgrunn, altså et stivt og ganske konservativt dansk-norsk, knyttet til det skrevne ord, er det imponerende at Rosendahl begav seg ut i dagligtalens ulendte farvann. Stavemåten viser enda trekk av skriftspråket, men stort sett er den så lik immigrantspråket at leserne må ha følt det som en stor befrielse. Her kunne utvandrerne kjenne seg selv igjen, eller kanskje snarere naboen. «Dette er ikke språket til presten og læreren» kunne de si. «Dette er vår måte å snakke på, den er hjemlig og morsom, den er vår.» Det høytidelige ble avløst av det hverdagslige.

3

Ola og Per utmerket seg fra starten ved at de snakket dialekt, ikke bokspråk. Bare måten navnene deres blir presentert på — «Han Ola» og «Han Per» er alment utbredt i norske dialekter: et personnavn måtte ha et bestemmelsesord for kjønn foran — *han* for menn, *ho* eller *hu* for kvinner. Ettersom disse formene ikke er brukelige i vanlig skriftspråk eller dannet dagligtale i byene, gir det navnene god folkelig klang. Stumme bokstaver blir sløyfet, uten at det har noe å si for uttalen, som når Rosendahl skriver *de* for *det* eller *huse* for *huset*. Dette er blitt kalt «øye-dialekt», da det bare registreres av øyet, som når engelske skribenter erstatter *though* med *tho,* eller *clothes* med *clo'es.* Talen innfører også former som er karakteristiske for folkemålet, f.eks. diftonger som *ei* for *e* i *veit* for *vet*; *au* for *ø* i *skaut* for *skjøt;* og *øi* (nå *øy*) i *øi* for *ø,* eller *høire* for *høre.* Diftongene ble brukt eller anbefalt i offisielle rettskrivningsreformer, men blant emigrantene ble disse formene følt som rare og fornøyelige. Det var som å høre en dommer i Høyesterett i Amerika si former som «ain't» eller «he don't».

Men Rosendahl gjorde mer enn bare å plassere skikkelsene sine på landsbygda hvor de fleste av dem hørte hjemme, i Norge som i Amerika. Han gav hver av dem en egen identitet ved å utstyre dem med forskjellige dialekter. Den konsekvens og dyktighet dette er gjennomført med, viser at han selv må ha behersket flere norske dialekter, foruten at han kunne skriftlig og muntlig norsk riksspråk.

Det er et markert skille i norsk talemål mellom midlandsdialektene i fjellbygdene og Østlandsdialektene på flatbygdene. Når vi ser på talemålsformene til Ola og Per, finner vi at de konsekvent bruker forskjellige former. Formene viser at Ola er fra en fjellbygd og Per er fra en av flatbygdene på Østlandet. En tilsvarende motsetning finnes i Skottland mellom «the highlander» og «the lowlander».

	Ola (fjellbygd)	Per (flatbygd)
«Jeg»	*e*	*je*
«Hun»	*ho*	*hu*
«Hun» (svaktrykk)	*'o*	*'a*
«Vi»	*me*	*vi*
«De»	*dei*	*dom*

Foruten disse forskjellene i bruk av pronomen, er det forskjell i visse adverbformer:

«Ikke»	intje (inkje)	itte
«Hvordan»	køs	haas
«Hva»	ko, kø	haa

I hvert tilfelle avviker fjellbygdsformene mest fra talemålet i byene, mens det er større overensstemmelse mellom fjellbygdsformene og gammelnorsk (eller nynorsken som ble skapt av Ivar Aasen i 1850-årene på grunnlag av de mer konservative dialektene).

Av og til opptrer forskjellene i en og samme samtale. I tegneserie 5 sier Per til Ola: «*Holdt i rompa paa 'a*» og Ola svarer: «*E ska nok hald 'o i rova e*». Her har vi *holdt* vs *hald; rompa* vs *rova;* det personlige pronomenet *'a* vs *'o*. Et av målmerkene i norske dialekter er formen på bestemt form hunkjønn, motsetningen *-i* vs *-a:* Ola bruker ofte *-i*, Per nesten alltid *-a,* jfr *höndi* (30); *øksi* (10); *fili* (11); *eika* (2); *møkka* (32). Ola har en flertallsform som er spesielt slående: *føtadn* (føttene); *grisidn* (grisene). Tilsvarende endelser for Per er *-an* eller bare *-a: tankan* (25); *kalva* (40). Ola bruker av og til flertallsformer av verb: *sko* (skal, 7); *leva* (leve, 12), det gjør aldri Per. Ola har vokalskifte (omlyd) i presens av sterke verb, f.eks. *fær* (får, 19, 26); *slær* (slår, 35), det har ikke Per, f.eks. *faar* (25, 32). Disse eksemplene kunne mangfoldiggjøres, men overlates hermed til leseren.

I én serie forteller Ola og Per oss at avisens abonnenter har lurt på hvor de kommer fra. De later som om de slår opp i oppslagsbøker og leksika, og kommer til at besteforeldrene var gorillaer. At det her gjøres litt narr av utviklingslæren betyr ikke at Rosendahl var uvitende om hvor personene hans kom fra. Det er tydelig, ikke bare ut fra språkformene, men også ut fra vårt kjennskap til hans familiebakgrunn og det samfunn han kom fra. Spring Grove var ett av områdene jeg undersøkte den gangen jeg forsket i nordmenns talespråk i Amerika.[9] De fleste jeg møtte der kom fra to områder: enten fra fjellbygda Hallingdal, eller fra flatbygda Hadeland. Vår kunstner har familie-

and family background. When I was doing field work on the speech of Norwegians in America, Spring Grove was one of the areas studied.[9] Nearly all the speakers I met there came from one of two areas: the mountain valley of Hallingdal or the lowland area of Hadeland. The farm name Rosendahl, from which our artist has his family cognomen, is in Brandbu parish in Hadeland. His wife was born of stock from Hallingdal and no doubt spoke that dialect.[10] Checking in Norwegian sources on the respective dialects has confirmed that in major features the two speakers do represent these localities.[11]

Of what significance is this choice of dialect in the economy of the strip? It is evident that Ola and Per communicate without difficulty and that they never comment unfavorably on the other's speech. Yet once Rosendahl had conceived the idea of two characters, one short and stocky, the other tall and lanky, with the former having the good sense, and the latter being a fantast, it was almost inevitable to pick the dialect of Hallingdal for the former and Hadeland for the latter. Hallingdal was a conservative area, in customs, costumes, and speech, with the kind of solid yeoman stock that populated its scanty and hard-worked soil. Hadeland was a more prosperous area, with larger farms and well-to-do owners who depended on a class of farm laborers to do much of their work. It was closer to Oslo, less conservative, more open to novel ideas propagated by the industrial revolution. Since speech forms are different in direct proportion to the amount of communication between their speakers, Hallingdal is the more untouched, the more picturesque, the more "genuine" of the two. It is therefore no coincidence that Ola is a Halling, while Per is a Hadelending: the interplay between them is the more amusing because of the sense that this reflects their basic personalities. It may not be entirely a coincidence that one Iver Lynne from Hadeland spent twenty years in America, including some time in the Spring Grove neighborhood, returning in 1928 to Norway. He made himself notorious as an inventor and fantast, who tried to make a perpetual motion machine.[12]

The third male character to make his entry is Per's brother, Lars, who arrives in Spring Grove in strip 20 (November 5, 1920). As a lowly "newcomer," the current equivalent of a "greenhorn," Lars surprisingly speaks upper class Norwegian, the "élite" dialect. As Rosendahl writes it, it is not markedly different from the Dano-Norwegian language of his captions. Since he is Per's brother, one wonders why he does not speak like him, until we learn much later (100, March 2, 1923) that he has "studied" at the universities in Christiania (Oslo) and

Berlin.[13] Whatever learning he may have absorbed there is of small value in the American farm community, an experience that many an intellectual shared on emigration. He is shocked by the "speed" of American life; he does not understand simple farm terms like "whippletree." He is unable to hitch up a horse or to manage the reins. He is the target of merciless ridicule, which is made the more painful by his own arrogance. The distance he puts between himself and the speakers of rural dialect puts him in the class of the "uppity": only the preacher and the teacher had a "right" to talk like this. His word for 'not' is *ikke* and for 'I' is *jeg* (pronounced "yay"), contrasting with Ola's *inkje* and *e* or with Per's *itte* and *je*.

The interplay of language between the three men strongly supports the discoveries made in recent years about the social roles of language. We cannot open our mouths without in some degree revealing what kind of a person we are. Rosendahl has here put language to work to show up the "city slicker" who looks down on the "hick," and gives the finest qualities to the one with the most deviant, highland dialect.

4

So far women have played only a very minor role, surprisingly so for a farm community. Ola's wife, who speaks the same dialect as he, appears at the start (1, 8), but after that flits in and out, with little or no function.[14] Otherwise women appear only as the objects of Per's amorous pursuit, all in vain until he goes to Fargo, North Dakota, and brings back plump Polla to be his wife. At this point the completely unrelated episodes of the preceding four years are replaced by a mild plot structure. With Ola and Per's return from a "vacation" with their thrashing rig in North Dakota in December, 1922, a new era in their lives opens. We are not told how Per managed to attain his long-sought happiness, but Polla comes to play a large role in the rest of the strips.

Polla reveals that she is a city girl, probably born in America, since she speaks city Norwegian, just as Lars does. Like him she is ignorant of the techniques of farming: when asked to milk a cow, she tries to start it by cranking its tail as if it were a model T Ford (102). From time to time she drops into English, answering Per's Norwegian with a "Yes dear" (106). Per is kept busy meeting her demands for better food, a new house, a pony, etc. She rewards him by temper tantrums over his clumsy ways, and for a time even leaves him to go back to her mother, plunging him into gloom (112). Her speech in Norwegian takes on some

navnet sitt fra gården Rosendahl, i Brandbu på Hadeland. Slekten til kona hans var fra Hallingdal og hun snakket sikkert hallingmål.[10] Kontroll i norske kilder angående de respektive dialekter har bekreftet at de to skikkelsene i hovedtrekk hører hjemme på disse stedene.[11]

Hvilken betydning har så valget av dialekt når det gjelder tegneseriens oppbygning? Det er tydelig at Ola og Per forstår hverandre uten vanskelighet, og ingen av dem sier noe ufordelaktig om den andres talemål. Men i det øyeblikk Rosendahl fikk idéen om å bruke to personer: den ene kort og kraftig, den andre lang og hengslete, den ene fornuftig og den andre en drømmer, var det nesten uunngåelig å la den førstnevnte benytte hallingmål og den sistnevnte hadelandsmål. Hallingdal var et konservativt område i vaner, klesdrakt og språk, med en solid bondeslekt som dyrket den skrinne jorda. På Hadeland var bøndene mer velstående og gårdene var større. Eierne var avhengige av at mye av arbeidet ble utført av gårdsarbeidere. Hadeland er også nærmere Oslo, mindre konservativt og mer åpent for nye idéer som fulgte i kjølvannet til den industrielle revolusjon. Talemålsformer varierer etter graden av kommunikasjon mellom brukerne, så Hallingdal er mest uberørt og pittoresk, det stedet som er det «ekteste» av de to. Det er derfor ingen tilfeldighet at Ola er halling, mens Per er hadelending. Samspillet dem i mellom er desto mer fornøyelig, fordi målformene er uttrykk for personligheter. Det har en viss interesse at en hadelending som het Iver Lynne bodde tyve år i Amerika, for en tid i nærheten av Spring Grove, før han drog tilbake til Norge i 1928. Han forsøkte å lage en evighetsmaskin og gjorde seg derved herostratisk berømt som oppfinner og drømmer.[12]

Tredjemann på arenaen er Pers bror Lars som kommer til Spring Grove i tegneserie 20 (5. november 1920). Lars er en grønn «nykommer», men han snakker overraskende nok norsk dannet dagligtale. Slik Rosendahl gjengir det, skiller det seg lite fra den dansk-norsken han bruker i overskriftene. Ettersom han er broren til Per lurer vi på hvorfor han ikke snakker samme dialekt som Per, inntil vi finner ut (100, 2. mars 1923) at han har «studert» ved universitetet, både i Kristiania (Oslo) og i Berlin.[13] Den lærdommen han eventuelt tilegnet seg på disse stedene er av liten verdi i det amerikanske bondesamfunnet. Det er en erfaring mange intellektuelle gjorde da de emigrerte. Lars er rystet over farten i det amerikanske samfunn; han skjønner ikke enkle gårdsuttrykk som «whippletree» (svingel). Han greier verken å spenne for en hest eller mestre tømmene. Han blir til latter, og er dertil arrogant. Ved at han holder avstand mellom seg selv og dem som snakker dialekt, plasserer han seg høyere på den sosiale rangstigen — det var bare presten og læreren som hadde «rett» til å snakke slik. Han sier *ikke* og *jeg* i motsetning til Olas *inkje* og *e* og Pers *itte* og *je*.

Det språklige samspillet mellom disse tre mennene bekrefter senere tids forskning angående språkets sosiale rolle. Vi kan ikke si svært mye uten at vi samtidig røper noe av vår bakgrunn. Rosendahl har her benyttet språket for å utlevere «bylapsen» som ser ned på «bondeknølen», og det er den som snakker det bygdemålet som avviker mest fra bymålet som han har utstyrt med de beste karakteregenskapene.

4

Kvinner har hittil spilt en veldig beskjeden rolle i serien. Det er overraskende, tatt i betraktning av at dette er et bondesamfunn. I begynnelsen møter vi kona til Ola, som snakker samme slags dialekt som ham (1, 8), men senere ser vi henne bare av og til, og hun synes ikke å ha noen spesiell funksjon.[14] Så en tid er kvinnene bare til stede som objekter for Pers kvinnejakt. Denne jakten er mislykket, inntil han drar til Fargo i Nord-Dakota og får med seg hjem trinne Polla som kone. Episodene har hittil ikke vært bundet sammen på noe vis, men heretter er de knyttet sammen ved hjelp av enkle intriger. Da Ola og Per kommer tilbake etter å ha reist på ferie til Nord-Dakota med skurtreskeren sin i desember 1922, begynner en ny epoke i deres liv. Vi får ikke høre hvordan Per endelig oppnådde den lykken han så lenge hadde søkt, men Polla kommer til å spille en betydelig rolle i resten av tegneserien.

Polla viser at hun er byjente, antagelig født i Amerika, dette fordi hun snakker norsk bymål, omtrent som Lars. Som han vet hun ingenting om gårdsdrift: når hun blir bedt om å melke ei ku, prøver hun å gjøre det ved å sveive på halen som om det skulle være en T-ford (102). Hun snakker ofte engelsk og svarer Per, som snakker norsk, med «Yes dear» (106). Per får det travelt med å etterkomme hennes krav om bedre mat, nytt hus, ponny osv. Hun belønner ham med temperamentsfulle utfall fordi han er så klossete. Hun forlater ham til og med en stund og reiser tilbake til moren sin og styrter ham derved ut i det dypeste mørke (112). Etter hvert blir hennes norsk delvis merket av Pers østnorske dialekt, f.eks. *beina dine* istedenfor *dine ben* og *je* istedenfor *jeg*. Når de kysser og kjæler sier hun: «Bare jeg kan være med dig, Per, saa er det all right» (98). Men når hun blir sint på ham sier hun: «Je ska lære dig, din laban» (114).

Det varer ikke lenge før nok en kvinne dukker opp. Det er

of Per's East Norwegian dialect when she says *beina dine* for *dine ben* 'your feet' and *je* for her usual *jeg* (i.e. *jei*) 'I'. When they bill and coo, she says, "Bare jeg kan være med dig, Per, saa er det allright" (If only I can be with you, Per, it's all right 98). But when she gets annoyed with him, she says "Je ska lære dig, din laban" (I'll teach you, you scoundrel 114).

Before long another woman is introduced into the ménage, Polla's mother, a hard-working, hatched-faced woman who bears only the name of "Værmor," i.e. "Mother-in-law," a dialect substitute for the urban "Svigermor" (which is used in some of the captions e.g. 164). Her language is similar to Per's lowland Norwegian. When Per accidentally peppers her instead of the old rooster with shot, she cries out, "Er du gæln da man! Kan du itte sjaa forskjæl paa beina mine aa ein gamal hane?" (Are you crazy, man? Can't you see the difference between my legs and an old rooster? 167). The forms *gæln* 'crazy', *itte* 'not', *sjaa* 'see', *beina* 'the legs' and *gamal* 'old' identify her speech as East Norwegian, contrary to Oslo standard like Lars' *(gal, ikke, se, bena, gammel)*. The lowland speech fits well with her mannish behavior. Surprisingly, Lars takes to courting her (228, 234), but we have to infer their marriage by his beginning to call her his wife (250).

One of the few happy events in Per's life is the birth of a daughter (217), who comes to be called Dada (e.g., 498). When she starts talking, her speech is the Norwegian of her parents, not surprisingly, but it can also be pure English. At first she is even presented with "baby-talk" features, e.g. *splut* for *sprut* 'spurt', *bettemor* for *bestemor* 'grandmother' (415).[15]

5

While the Norwegian dialects spoken by the characters are relics of their past, the most conspicuous feature of their language is the vivid interaction with English, the language of their future. There is no serious difference in this respect between Ola and Per, while Lars, at least in his newcomer days, is still untouched by the new language. Over the seventeen years that Rosendahl drew his comic strip, there is a conspicuous increase in the amount of English spoken. This is most noticeable with Polla and her daughter Dada. In a conversation over the telephone Polla switches back and forth in the manner of bilinguals who are completely at ease in both languages and have no inhibitions about maintaining a single standard.[16] When Rosendahl began drawing in 1918, the anti-foreign campaign was in full swing in America, and by 1935 its effects were clearly noticeable.[17] In his last cartoon of 1935, which was also the last in the series, Rosendahl shipped his characters off to Norway by plane. But one wonders just how well they would be understood in the homeland after their linguistic acculturation to America.

Newcomer Lars is the butt of all jokes because he even fails to understand the English words that have been incorporated into his countrymen's Norwegian. From the point of view of such immigrants, who have had to go through the experience of being a "newcomer," it was no fun. My informants have told me of how stupid they felt at not understanding what seemed to be Norwegian, even their own dialect of it, and yet being baffled by such everyday terms as *fence, barn, shed,* or *shanty.* They were told to *fix* something or *make* something, but stood there quite helpless.[18]

Likewise Lars is unable to deduce the meaning of *hyppeltræ,* which sounds for all the world like a Norwegian word, but is quite unknown in Norway. He does not know that it is an adaptation of English *whippletree,* and assuming it must be some kind of tree, goes to the woods to find it (28).[19] Soon, however, he learns, at least enough to become a devotee of what he learns to call a *jaagg,* the American-Norwegian version of *jug,* replacing Norwegian *dunk.* Later on he claims that he has never had anything in it but *malassi* 'molasses' (588), but his inebriated actions belie the claim. See the charming strip where he falls on one side of the fence and his jug on the other. As the contents trickle out, he moans: "I hear your voice, but I can't help you" (148).[20]

Ola and Per are already sufficiently acculturated to feel no hesitation about adopting English words in their Norwegian speech. For the most part they are probably quite unaware of doing so. This is especially noticeable in their use of interjections. As is well known, these are the first items to be picked up by foreign learners, since they require no knowledge of the grammar of the new language, and they are highly expressive of attitudes and emotions that would be hard to translate. From the early strips we can pick up a whole flora of such terms: *hello, goodbye, whoa, giddap, hurry up, well, yes sirree, go ahead, you bet, all ready, come on, by jiminy, by thunder, my goodness, say, never you mind, go on, son of a gun, yes man, oh golly, uh-huh, gee whiz, shucks, sick 'em* etc. Today many of these gain flavor by having become old-fashioned or rural. Of course Ola and Per also retain many Norwegian expressions of the same type: *au* 'ow, ouch', *ja* 'yes' and *nei* 'no', used to introduce sentences (rather like 'well' in English), the much quoted

Pollas mor, et arbeidsjern av en kvinne med smalt, skarpt ansikt. Hun blir bare kalt «Værmor», dialektordet for «svigermor» (som hun kalles i noen av overskriftene, f.eks. 164). Hennes språk ligner på Pers Hadelandsdialekt. Da Per ved en feiltagelse skyter på henne istedenfor på den gamle hanen roper hun: «Er du gæln da man! Kan du itte sjaa forskjæl paa beina mine aa ein gamal hane?» (167). Formene *gæln, itte, sjaa, beina* og *gamal* står i motsetning til byformene som Lars bruker *(gal, ikke, se, bena, gammel)*. Hadelandsdialekten passer godt til hennes mannhaftige opptreden. Overraskende nok begynner Lars å gjøre kur til henne (228, 234), og vi må slutte oss til at de har giftet seg når han begynner å omtale henne som sin kone (250).

Et av de få lykkelige øyeblikk i Pers liv er da første datteren blir født (217). Hun blir kalt Dada (f.eks. 498). Det er ikke overraskende at hun snakker norsk som foreldrene når hun begynner å snakke, men hun lærer snart et rent engelsk. Aller først snakker hun babyspråk, f.eks. *splut* (sprut), *bettemor* (bestemor) (415).[15]

5

Mens personenes norske dialekter stammer fra deres fortid, er engelsk, fremtidens språk, det mest påfallende nye ved språket de bruker. Når det gjelder innslaget av engelsk, er det ikke noen markert forskjell mellom Ola og Per, mens Lars fremdeles er upåvirket av engelsk, iallfall i den første tiden. I løpet av de 17 årene Rosendahl utarbeidet tegneserien, er det påfallende hvordan omfanget av engelsk økte. Dette kommer tydeligst til uttrykk hos Polla og datteren Dada. Bare i én telefonsamtale veksler Polla frem og tilbake mellom engelsk og norsk slik tospråklige kan gjøre det når de behersker begge språk og ikke legger vekt på å holde fast ved det ene språket.[16] Da Rosendahl begynte å tegne i 1918 var kampanjen mot fremmedspråk i full sving i Amerika, og i 1935 kunne virkningen av den tydelig merkes.[17] I den siste serien i 1935, som avsluttet hans virke, sendte Rosendahl personene sine med fly til Norge. En kan lure på hvor godt de ville blitt forstått i hjemlandet, deres lingvistiske tilpasning til amerikanske forhold tatt i betraktning.

Nykommeren Lars blir alltid gjort narr av fordi han ikke engang forstår de engelske ordene som er blitt en del av norsken til de andre. Fra disse senere innvandrernes synspunkt, dvs. de som måtte erfare hva det ville si å være en «nykommer», var det ikke alltid så morsomt. Noen jeg har snakket med, har fortalt meg hvor dumme de følte seg når de ikke forstod det som hørtes

ut til å være norsk, til og med på deres egen dialekt, og allikevel ble de forvirret av dagligdagse ord som *fence, barn, shed,* eller *shanty.* De ble bedt om å *fixe* noe eller *make* noe, og ble stående helt hjelpeløse.[18]

På samme måte er Lars ute av stand til å finne ut hva *hyppeltræ* betyr. Det høres ut som et norsk ord, men det er helt ukjent i Norge. Han vet ikke at ordet skriver seg fra det engelske «whippletree» (svingeltre) og antar derfor at det må være en tresort. Han drar følgelig til skogs for å finne det (28).[19] Snart lærer han imidlertid nok til å bli glad i det han kaller for en *jaagg*. Dette er den norsk-amerikanske versjonen av *jug*, som altså betyr en norsk *dunk* (med brennevin i). Senere hevder han at han bare har *malassi* (molasses) i den (588), men det han gjør i påvirket tilstand forteller noe annet. Jfr. den sjarmerende serien (61) hvor han faller på den ene siden av gjerdet og dunken på den andre. Mens innholdet renner ut, jamrer han: «Jeg hører stemmen din, men jeg kan ikke hjelpe deg» (148).[20]

Ola og Per har allerede tilpasset seg amerikanske forhold slik at de ikke betenker seg på å bruke engelske ord i norsken. Stort sett er de vel ikke klar over at de gjør det. Dette er særlig merkbart når det gjelder bruken av interjeksjoner. Som alle vet, er utrop noe av det første som blir plukket opp av dem som skal lære et fremmed språk. En grunn er at de ikke krever kjennskap til fremmedspråkets grammatikk, en annen at de gir uttrykk for holdninger og følelser som er vanskelige å oversette. Det er en mengde slike utrop i de første tegneseriene: *hello, goodby, whoa, giddap, hurry up, well, yes sirree, go ahead, you bet, all ready, come on, by jiminy, by thunder, my goodness, say, never you mind, go on, son of a gun, yes mam, oh golly, uh-huh, gee whiz, shucks, sick 'em* osv. I dag er disse ordene enda mer komiske, delvis er de blitt gammeldagse og delvis forbinder man dem med en tapt landlig kultur. Ola og Per fortsetter også selvfølgelig å bruke mange norske uttrykk av samme type: *au; ja* og *nei* for å innlede setninger på samme måte som 'well' på engelsk; *uff; du store verden; aa, aa ja, aa nei; hei gut; aa nei da; jo da; pas dig; jasaa; se der; har du set sligt?* Man finner også småbanning som: *gud forsyne mig* (5) og skjellsord som *din elendige idiot* (6), eller uttrykk for avsky: *tvi* eller *tvi vori* (40).

Substantiv er den ordklassen som vanligst blir tatt opp i norsken. Dette gjelder gjerne, om ikke alltid, navn på ting eller idéer som emigrantene ikke kjente til eller ikke hadde brukt på landsbygda i hjemlandet. Teoretisk kan ethvert ord bli overført fra ett språk til et annet, men det behøver nødvendigvis ikke skje. Det koster mindre å overta det ordet som er i vanlig bruk

uff 'oh dear', *du store verden* 'good heavens', *aa (aa ja, aa nei)* 'oh (yes, no)', *hei gut* 'hey man', *aa nei daa* 'oh no', *jo da* 'oh yes', *pas dig* 'look out', *jasaa* 'is that so', *se der* 'look', *ha du set sligt* 'ever see anything like it?' There are also mild oaths like *gud forsyne mig* 'god help me' (5) and terms of abuse like *din elendige idiot* 'you miserable idiot' (6) or of disgust like *tvi* or *tvi vori* 'pfui' (40).

Nouns are the next most common type of word adopted from English. These are usually, but not necessarily, names of objects or ideas not known to or used by rural emigrants in the homeland. In theory any word can be transferred from one language to another, and equally no word absolutely needs to be. But taking over the word that is customary in the dominant English-speaking world is less effort than making up one's own or even trying to recall an old-world term that is rarely heard.

The era of Rosendahl's strip was most typically the period when cheap automobiles first became available, along with an abundance of motorized farm machinery. So it is not surprising to find the strip teeming with English words for motors and motoring. In fact, the strips most appropriately open with Ola's getting his first car. The word appears in a form (also well known in American Swedish) derived from the plural, used in a singular meaning: *en kars* 'a car', *karsen* 'the car' (1). In the early strips we meet other machine products like *blower, force feeder, switch, brake, throttle, thrashing rig, high* (gear), and *radiator cap.* The men who work a thrashing rig constitute a *crew.* The landscape is cut up into *fields (ei fil,* pl. *filer),* often in units of forty acres known as "forties." Small towns have such things as a (railroad) *depot* and *sidewalks.* Innovations in social life are the *picnic,* the *business,* and the *teacher* (in the English school; the Norwegian teacher is a *lærer).* Older Norwegian terms of measure are similar in sound, and they become American by being given American values: *fot* 'foot', *mil* 'mile', *pund* 'pound', *daler* 'dollar' (all from before the adoption in Norway of the metric system).

Among the natural features of the land that the settlers met were new animals like the *skunk,* new trees like the *butternut* and the *basswood oak,* and climatic traumas like the *cyclone.* In coping with their new mechanical equipment they had to learn to *fix* things and to *handle* machinery: belts could *slip* and *jump the cog,* and chutes could get *clogged up.* Lars was not the only one who had to learn to *start up* and to *hurry up,* in this new land of *speed.* There were plenty of problems to *bother* them, including even that they had to *board* the teacher.

In the daily speech of our characters such words as the above tended in general to be accepted as if they were native Norwegian words.[21] To the student of language there is nothing peculiar or unusual about this, but to the average reader and speaker it may give a comic effect. They are often not aware of the widespread practice of word borrowing, although their own English is full of words derived from Latin and French, or even from the Norse of the Vikings. We may also call the process "importation" or "transfer," whereby the new word is naturalized into the language by acquiring a native set of sounds and grammatical forms.

Rosendahl represents the Norwegian-American words by rewriting them into Norwegian spelling. His practice here is not consistent, since he often lets the English words retain their spelling. But he respells them often enough to give the reader the delightful effort of trying to reconstruct the speakers' actual pronunciation.[22]

Here are a few samples to show his practice. The vowel *a* of *all right* and *call* he spells *aa* (now written *å*) for a sound between *oh* and *aw: aalreit* (5), *aal reddi* (6), *kaale* (27). The fronted *a* of *cap* becomes *æ* (its nearest equivalent) in *redietorkæppen* (8), but *a* (like *ah*) in *basvoddtræ* (2), and even *ei* in *yeinki* (9). The *a* of *brake* could become *e,* short as in *brekk* (1), long as in *redietorkæppen* (8). The diphthongal *i* of right could become either *ei,* as in *aalreit* (1), *seidvaaka* (14), or *ai* as in *godbai, saiklon, hai* (all in 1), *bai tønder* (7). The difficult (for Norwegians) sound of *u* in *skunk* became *aa* in *skaank* (2), but *ö (ø)* in *bai tönder* (7) and *trökk* (26). Vowels that had little stress were often lost, as in *gaa hed* (2) from *go ahead.*

Certain English consonants offered Norwegians problems, e.g. *th, w, j* and *z.* The voiceless *th* (as in *think*) became *t,* as in *tratel* (1), *bai tønder* (7), while the voiced *th* (as in *this*) usually became *d,* as in *wid* (2), *badra* (19). *W* was replaced by *v,* as in *basvod* (2), or *Vaterloryggen* (8) (Waterloo Ridge). But in the combination of *wh-* before *i,* Norwegians heard it as *hy,* so that *whippletree* became *hyppeltræ* (28). English *j* was replaced by Norwegian *j,* a consonantal *y*-sound, where the spelling prevailed (e.g. *jompe* 'jump'), otherwise by nearsounding combinations like *dj* or even in the word *partridge* by *s: patris* (75). Similarly *ch* could become *ts,* as in *svits* (1). The sound *z* (often written *s* in English) invariably became *s,* as in *bisness* (6). It is evident from the examples of complete English sentences spoken by Ola and Per that they did not master English pho-

blant engelsktalende, enn å lage et nytt selv, eller prøve å huske et ekte norsk ord som sjelden blir hørt lenger.

Rosendahls tegneserie ble skapt på den tid da billige biler kom i handelen i Amerika. Samtidig ble det vanlig med motoriserte landbruksredskaper. Derfor er det ikke overraskende at det kryr av engelske ord og uttrykk som har med motorer og bilkjøring å gjøre i tegneserien. Serien starter faktisk med at Ola får den første bilen sin. Ordet forekommer i en form (også velkjent i svensk-amerikansk), avledet fra flertall, men brukt i entallsbetydning: *en kars* (a car), *karsen* (the car) (1). I de første tegneseriene finner vi andre maskinprodukter som *blower* (blåsemaskin); *force feeder* (tvangsforingsmaskin); *switch* (bryter); *brake* (bremse); *throttle* (gasspedal); *thrashing rig* (skurtresker); *high* (om gear); og *radiator cap* (radiatorlokk). Mennene som jobbet med skurtreskeren utgjør et *crew*. Jorden blir delt opp i *fields* (ei *fil*, pl. *filer*), ofte enheter som bestod av førti *acres* (ca. 120 mål) og ble kalt *førtier*. Småbyene hadde *railroad depot* (jernbanestasjoner) og *sidewalks* (fortau). Nyskapninger i det sosiale liv var *picnic, business* og *teacher* (i engelsk skole; den norske læreren kaltes *lærer*). Eldre norske måleenheter har en lydkvalitet som minner om amerikansk, og de ble amerikanske ved at de fikk nye verdier: *fot* (foot); *mil* (mile); *pund* (pound); *daler* (dollar), fra før det metriske system ble innført i Norge.

I naturen møtte nybyggerne ukjente dyr som *skunk* (stinkdyr), ukjente trær som *butternut og basswood oak,* samt klimatiske mareritt som *the cyclone.* For å beherske det nye mekaniske utstyret måtte de lære å *fix* forskjellige ting og *handle* maskiner: Drivremmer (belts) kunne *slip* og *jump the cog,* og sjakter (chutes) kunne bli *clogged up.* Lars var ikke den eneste som måtte lære å *starte up* og å *hurry up* i dette nye fartens land (country of *speed*). Det var mange problemer som kunne *badre* (plage) dem, de måtte til og med kanskje *borde teachern* = gi læreren hus og mat.

6

Slike ord ble stort sett akseptert som opprinnelige norske ord i våre personers dagligtale.[21] For en språkforsker er ikke dette noe rart eller uvanlig, men det kan virke komisk på vanlige lesere. De er ofte ikke klar over hvor alminnelig det er å ta opp fremmedord i språket, selv om deres eget språk vrimler av ord som stammer fra engelsk, tysk, latin og fransk. Engelsk har til og med vært utsatt for nordisk påvirkning i vikingtiden. Denne prosessen kan også kalles «import» eller «overføring», da nye ord som regel blir tilpasset språkets lydsystem og morfologi.

Rosendahl gjengir de norsk-amerikanske ordene ved å omskrive dem til norsk stavemåte. Dette er ikke gjort konsekvent, ofte lar han engelske ord beholde sin stavemåte. Men han omskriver dem ofte nok til å gi leseren gleden av å prøve å rekonstruere den opprinnelige uttalen til den som snakker.[22]

Her er noen eksempler som viser hvordan han gjorde det. Vokalen *a* i *all right* og *call* gjengir han *aa* (nå *å*) for lyden mellom *oh* og *aw*: *aalreit*(5), *aal reddi* (6), *kaale* (27). *A* i *cap* blir *æ* som i *redietorkæppen* (8) men *a* i *basvoddtræ* (2) og *ei* i *yeinki* (9). *A* i *brake* kunne bli kort *e* i *brekk* (1) og lang *e* i *redietorkæppen* (8). Diftongisk *i* i *right* kunne bli enten *ei* som i *aalreit* (1), *seidvaaka* (14), eller *ai* som i *godbai, saiklon, hai* (alle i 1), *bai tønder* (7). *U*-lyden i *skunk* (som er vanskelig for nordmenn) blir *aa* i *skaank* (2), men *ö* (*ø*) i *bai tönder* (7) og *trökk* (26). Trykklette vokaler ble ofte ikke uttalt, som i *gaa hed* (2) fra *go ahead*.

Visse engelske konsonanter var problematiske for nordmenn, f.eks. *th, w, j* og *z*. Ustemt *th* (som i *think*) ble *t*, som i *tratel* (1), *bai tønder* (7), mens stemt *th* (som i *this*) vanligvis ble *d*, som i *wid* (2), *badra* (19). *W* ble erstattet av *v*, som i *basvod* (2), eller *Vaterloryggen* (8) (Waterloo Ridge). Men kombinasjonen *wh* + *i* ble oppfattet av nordmenn som *hy*, og *whippletree* ble *hyppeltræ* (28). Engelsk *j* ble erstattet med den norske j-lyden, men her kommer forskjellen ikke alltid til uttrykk i stavemåten *(jompe = jump)*. Engelsk *j* ble også erstattet med lignende lyder som *dj*, eller til og med *s,* som i *partridge (patris,* 75). På samme måte kunne *ch* bli *ts*, som i *svits* (1). Z-lyden (som ofte skrives *s* på engelsk) ble alltid uttalt *s*, som i *bisness* (6). Det fremgår av de engelske setningene Ola og Per sier at de ikke behersket engelsk fonetikk og grammatikk, f.eks. *ay tank so* (47) for *I think so*. Et annet sikkert tegn på at det engelske ordet er blitt integrert i det norske systemet, er at det tar opp norske endelser.[23] Alle verbene får riktig form. Infinitiver ender på *-e* (i dialektene finner vi enten *-e* eller *-a*): *Treppe* (trap) (2); *starte* (start, 6); *borde* (board, 11); *teache* (teach, 11); *handle* (handle, 15); *feede* (feed, 16); *toppe* (top, 18); *kaale* (call, 27) osv. Fortidsformer ender på *-a*: *badra* (bothered, 19); *jompa* (jumped, 19); *cleana* (cleaned, 23); *hæpna* (happened, 25); *shippa* (shipped, 16). Likeså partisipper: *upclogga* (clogged up, 19); *strippa* (stripped), *chænga* (changed, 26), *kætja* (caught, 37). Presensendelsen er *-a* (i Olas dialekt) eller *-er* (i Pers dialekt): *feela* (feels, 25); *loser* (loses, 15).

Substantivets tre kjønn blir opprettholdt, men låneordenes fordeling på kjønn er ikke konsekvent. Artikkelen *ein* markerer

netics or grammar, e.g. *ay tank so* (47) for *I think so*.

Another sure sign of integration of the English word into the Norwegian system is its adopting Norwegian endings from Norwegian grammar.[23] All verbs acquire appropriate forms. Infinitives end in *-e* (the dialects can have either *-e* or *-a): treppe* 'trap' (2), *starte* 'start' (6), *borde* 'board' (11), *teache* 'teach' (11), *handle* 'handle' (15), *feede* 'feed' (16), *toppe* 'top' (18), *kaale* 'call' (27) etc. Past tenses and participles end in *-a: badra* 'bothered' (19), *jompa* 'jumped' (19), *cleana* 'cleaned' (23), *hæpna* 'happened' (25), *shippa* 'shipped' (16); (participles) *upclogga* 'clogged up' (19), *strippa* 'stripped', *chænga* 'changed' (26), *kætja* 'caught' (37). Present tenses end in *-a* (in Ola's dialect) or *-er* (in Per's): *feela* 'feels' 25, *loser* 'loses' 15.

Nouns are assigned one of three genders, unknown in English, but usually required in Norwegian, though the loanwords may vacillate: masculine, feminine, or neuter. The m. is marked by the article *ein* 'a', suffixed *-(e)n* 'the' singular, *-adn* (Ola)/*-an, -a* (Per) 'the' plural. The f. is marked by *ei, -a* (also *-i* in Ola's dialect), and *-idn* (Ola)/*-en* (Per). The n. is marked by *eit, -e,* and *-a.* Most nouns are given masculine gender: *svitsen* (1), *trateln* (1), *ingen bisnes* (6), *brekken* (8), *redieterkæppen* (8), *depon* (11), *teacher'n* (12), *ingen trik* (14), *ein log* (22), *vaterlevel'n* (23), *jaaggen* (33); in the plural *dentistadn* 'the dentists' (35), *blanksadn* 'the blanks' (47) (with a plural). The nouns occurring in this material that are feminine are *crewa* (19) (usually written *krua*), *kønnfila* 'the corn field' (45) (Per), *potetfili* 'the potato field' (11) (Ola), *statefæra* 'the state fair' (36) (in the caption; the cartoon says *fairn,* both being in use). There are no neuter nouns in the early strips, but *staare* 'the store' occurs later (in *chain staare* 459). 'Corn' as neuter (e.g. *kaunne* 41) is of course a Norwegian word, though here with American meaning.

The attentive reader will also note some creative formations along with the simple importations.[24] A popular phrase with our characters is *det bitar grisen* (434), i.e. 'that beats everything', literally 'that beats the pig'. While the verb has to be English *beat,* there is no such phrase with the word *gris* 'pig' in either language. I can testify to the existence of the phrase in the immigrant community. There is also extensive word formation with compounds of English and Norwegian words, e.g. *Vateloryggen* 'Waterloo Ridge' (8), *skaankeskin* 'skunk hide' (2), *basvodeika* 'the basswood oak' (2), *ein halv førtivæg* 'half a forty's distance' (14), *uppklogga* 'clogged up' (19), *lombervögni* 'the lumber wagon' (26), *hyrejenta* 'the hired girl' (27), *snøbalbuska* 'the snowball bush' (27). Such compounds are evidence that the English words have become part of the language, and that we have true American Norwegian before us.

There are no false notes in this language: this is the true accent of the rural Norwegian immigrant and his descendants over the years.

7

I hope to have shown that Rosendahl had his eyes and ears open to the livelier aspects of Norwegian speech among his neighbors. He subtly embodied three major types of spoken Norwegian in their dialogues, and in so doing he reversed the homeland ordering of their status. The élite speech of Oslo and its upper middle class is spoken by the immigrant who makes the greatest fool of himself, and who seizes every chance to make a show of himself — Lars. Of the two rural dialects spoken, the Hallingdal dialect of Ola the highlander, which was by some looked down on as an especially uncouth dialect, is spoken by the most stable and sensible of the characters, stocky Ola with the overalls. The lowland East Norwegian, Per, is a fantast, caught between the fascinating mechanical fads of his time and a conspicuous lack of common sense. His half-urbanized dialect betrays his origin.

What about the future? As suggested earlier, Rosendahl reflects a growing anglicization, especially in the younger generation. Per's Fargo-born Polla can speak Norwegian, but at least from strip 368 (February 14, 1930) she nearly always speaks English. His daughter Dada speaks Norwegian to her grandmother (470), but mostly English to her parents (from 471, July 1, 1932). But grandmother, known as Værmor, brings on the scene her twin sister Cleopatra, who speaks only English (cf. 581, 589, March — May, 1935). This improbable character elopes with the black hired man named Julius Caesar (595), who is represented as speaking a kind of Amos-and-Andy black dialect.

The absurdity of this last episode in Ola and Per's epic may reflect dwindling powers of invention or a loss of interest in the strip. In any case it highlights the approaching end of the Norwegian-speaking era. Between 1918 and 1935 the percentage of Norwegian services in the Norwegian-Lutheran Church of America had fallen from 61.2 % to 25.7 %. By 1949 it was down to the infinitesimal number of 2.7.[25]

Taken as a whole, Rosendahl's strips have given us a delightful, if one-sided picture of immigrant life, part realistic, part fantasy. His use of English is also real, again somewhat

hankjønn, i bestemt form entall *-(e)n*. Bestemt form flertall: *-adn* (Ola)/*-an*, *-a* (Per). Artikkelen *ei* markerer hunkjønn, i bestemt form entall *-a* (Olas dialekt har også *-i*). Bestemt form flertall: *-idn* (Ola), *-en* (Per). Artikkelen *eit* markerer intetkjønn, *-e* og *-a*. De fleste substantiver havner i hankjønnskategorien: *svitsen* (1), *trateln* (1), *ingen bisnes* (6), *brekken* (8), *redieterkæppen* (8), *depon* (11), *teacher'n* (12), *ingen trik* (14), *ein log* (22), *vaterlevel'n* (23), *jaaggen* (33); i flertall *dentistadn* (tannlegene, 35), *blanksadn* (the blanks, 47). Hunkjønnsord som forekommer i dette materialet er: *crewa* (19) (vanligvis skrevet *krua*); *könnfila* (the corn field, 45) (Per); *potetfili* (the potato field, 11) (Ola); *statefæra* (the state fair, 36) (i overskriften; i talemålet *fairn,* begge deler brukes). Det er ingen intetkjønnsord i de første tegneseriene, men *staare* (the store) forekommer senere (i *chain staare,* 459). 'Corn' som intetkjønnsord (*kaunne,* 41) er selvfølgelig et norsk ord, selv om betydningen her er amerikansk.

Den oppmerksomme leser vil også ha lagt merke til noen nyskapninger ved siden av enkle låneord.[24] En frase som er populær blant personene våre er: *det bitar grisen* (434), dvs. 'det overgår alt' — bokstavelig — «det slår grisen». Verbet må være engelsk *beat* (slå), men det finnes ikke noen slik frase med ordet *gris* i noen av språkene. Jeg kan bevitne at frasen finnes i innvandrersamfunnet. Orddannelse ved hjelp av sammensetninger av engelske og norske ord forekommer også ofte, f.eks. *Vaterloryggen* (Waterloo Ridge, 8); *skaankeskin* (skunk hide, 2); *basvodeika* (the basswood oak, 2); *ein halv førtivæg* (half a forty's distance, 14); *upklogga* (clogged up, 19); *lombervögni* (the lumber wagon, 26); *hyrejenta* (the hired girl, 27); *snøbalbuska* (the snowball bush, 27). Slike sammensetninger er et bevis på at engelske ord er blitt en del av språket, og at vi står overfor ekte norsk-amerikansk.

Det er ingen falske toner i dette språket; det *er* eller *var* språkformen til innvandrerne fra landsbygda i Norge og deres etterkommere gjennom mange år.

7

Jeg har forhåpentlig påvist at Rosendahl var lydhør for de livligere aspektene ved den norsken han og naboene hans snakket. På en underfundig måte gjorde han bruk av tre hovedtyper av norsk talemål i dialogene og med det samme snudde han opp ned på rangordningen disse hadde i Norge. Elitespråket fra Oslo blir brukt av den innvandreren (Lars) som dummer seg mest ut og som griper enhver sjanse til å hevde seg. Av de to bygdemålene, er Hallingdialekten til Ola, som av mange ble sett ned på og ansett for å være mest bondsk, brukt av den mest stabile og fornuftige av personene — kraftige Ola med overallen. Per, fra flatbygdene i Øst-Norge, er drømmeren, fanget mellom tidens fascinerende nye mekaniske påfunn og en påfallende mangel på fornuft. Hans dialekt, nærmere bymålet, avslører hans bakgrunn.

Hva med fremtiden? Som tidligere antydet, avbildes her en økende anglisering, særlig for den yngre generasjons vedkommende. Pers kone Polla, som er født i Fargo, kan snakke norsk, men etter tegneserie 368 (14. februar 1930) snakker hun nesten alltid engelsk. Datteren Dada snakker norsk til bestemoren (470), men for det meste blir det engelsk til foreldrene (fra 471, 1. juli 1932).

De siste episodene i historien om Ola og Per er kanskje et utslag av en manglende evne til å finne på noe nytt, og av at Rosendahl hadde mistet interessen for tegneserien. De belyser ihvertfall avslutningen på den norsktalende epoken. I tiden mellom 1918 og 1935 hadde det prosentvise antall gudstjenester på norsk i den norsk-lutherske kirke i Amerika sunket fra 61,2% til 25,7%. I 1949 var tallet uendelig lite, bare 2,7%.[25]

Alt i alt har Rosendahls tegneserie gitt oss et herlig, om enn noe ensidig, bilde av innvandrerlivet, bygget delvis på realiteter, delvis på fantasi. Hans bruk av engelske gloser er også ekte, om kanskje litt overdrevet for effekten. Men det er vanskelig å sette fingeren på uttrykk som ikke var vanlige blant innbyggerne i Spring Grove i Minnesota, for ikke å si blant de fleste av midtvestens folk som stammet fra landsbygda i Norge.

NOTER

1 Lowells dialekt var uttrykksformen i hans *Bigelow Papers* (1848, 1867), mens dialekten til Harris var uttrykksformen i hans historier om *Uncle Remus* (1881).

2 Jfr. *The New Encyclopaedia Britannica* (1974) når det gjelder tegneserier i Amerika, særlig bind 3, side 920-22, med bibliografi.

3 Se O.S. Johnson, *Nybyggerhistorie* for detaljerte personalia om Spring Grove og det norske settlementet der.

4 Jfr. Odd Lovoll, 1977, om *Decorah-Posten;* «Han Ola og Han Per» blir omtalt s. 96-97. Jfr. også Einar Haugen, «Symra — A Memoir», i samme bind.

exaggerated by the nature of his medium. But it would be hard to put one's finger on any expression that could not have been heard among the citizens of Spring Grove, Minnesota, or for that matter by virtually any midwestern rural immigrant from Norway.

NOTES

1 Lowell's dialect was the vehicle of his *Bigelow Papers* (1848, 1867), while Harris's was his *Uncle Remus* stories (1881).
2 On the comic strip in the United States see *The New Encyclopædia Britannica* (1974), esp. vol. 3, pp. 920—22, with bibliography.
3 For detailed personal information on Spring Grove and its Norwegian settlements see O. S. Johnson, *Nybyggerhistorie.*
4 On *Decorah-Posten* see Odd Lovoll 1977; he specifically comments on "Han Ola og han Per" pp. 96—97. See also Einar Haugen, "Symra — A Memoir", in the same volume.
5 On Luther College see David T. Nelson, *Luther College* (1961).
6 For a full account of the language of the Norwegian immigrant, especially in the rural Midwest, see Haugen 1953.
7 On the Norwegian language controversy see Haugen 1966.
8 Lovoll, p. 98; Haugen 1953, pp. 148—9.
9 For my general impressions of the Spring Grove settlement, which I studied in 1942, see Haugen 1953, p. 614.
10 On Rosendahl's family background see O. S. Johnson, pp. 15 and 118.
11 On the dialect of Hallingdal see Kjell Venås, *Hallingmålet* (1977). There seems to be no monograph on the Hadeland dialect, but I am grateful for information given me by the personnel of Norsk Målførearkiv, Oslo. My personal informant was Oskar Holter, Lysaker, whom I hereby thank.
12 Information from Oskar Petter Jensrud of Harestua, Norway. The emigrant's name was Iver Lynne, b. 1885, emigrated 1908, returned 1928, after which he was known as "Iver Amerikaner".
13 Doubt is thrown on his intellectual eminence by Per's next remark, that he "gik sju aar for presten," i.e. that it took him seven years before the minister would admit him to confirmation, a process normally taking only one year (100).
14 The few times Ola's wife appeared, it is evident that she speaks the same (Hallingdal) dialect as he. Rosendahl's underplaying of her role is one of the strip's oddities. She returns from Norway (160), then leaves him for Minneapolis (231), comes back (542), but soon leaves for Norway (584).
15 Some incidental characters speak a Trönder dialect, e.g. a woman at Per's ski meet (*Æ trur æ gaar heim* 'I think I'll go home' 173) and two fishermen cutting ice on Lake Superior (*hi* 'have', *fingrain* 'the fingers', *kain* 'can' 211). Perhaps the wintry context suggested this more northerly dialect. There were speakers of Trönder on Waterloo Ridge when I visited the area.
16 Switching is a topic that has elicited great interest among recent students of bilingualism; cf. J. Nartey 1982 and references cited there. For a first definition and study of the phenomenon see Haugen 1953, p. 65.

17 For its effects on Norwegian see chapters 10 and 11 in Haugen 1953, esp. p. 255—260. For a general treatment of its midwestern effects see Luebke 1980.
18 See examples and discussion in Haugen 1953, 58—60.
19 The traditional spelling *whiffletree* (see Webster's *New International Dictionary* et al.) does not do justice to the usual midwestern pronunciation with *pp.* Apparently the association with the unknown verb *whiffle* has been replaced by *whip,* describing its mobility.
20 This anecdote also appears in O. S. Johnson, *Nybyggerhistorie,* p. 135, in reference to an unnamed drunkard: "Han hørte det lød kluk, kluk og da utbrøt han: 'Ja, jeg hører nok din røst, kjære vennen min, men jeg kan slet ikke hjælpe dig.'" (He heard it say 'drip, drip' and then he exclaimed: 'Yes, I hear your voice, dear friend, but I can't help you at all.') Rosendahl may have borrowed it from Johnson, his cartoon having appeared March 14, 1924, four years after the book; or it may have been common folklore in the community. Johnson writes a good deal about drinking in the Spring Grove community.
21 See Haugen 1953, chapter 16, on the phonology of loanwords.
22 The terminology here used is non-technical; for details see the previous reference.
23 On the grammatical adaptation of loanwords see Haugen 1953, chapter 17.
24 On the formation of new native words through borrowing see Haugen 1953, chapter 18.
25 Statistics in Haugen, 1953, 265—67, from the annual church reports.

BIBLIOGRAPHY

Haugen, Einar. *The Norwegian Language in America: A Study in Bilingual Behavior.* 2 vols. Philadelphia, Pa.: University of Pennsylvania Press, 1953. 2. ed. 1 vol., Bloomington, Ind.: Indiana University Press, 1964.

Haugen, Einar. *Language Conflict and Language Planning.* Cambridge, Mass.: Harvard University Press, 1966.

Haugen, Einar. "Symra: A Memoir." *Norwegian-American Studies* 27.101-110 (1977).

Johnson, O. S. *Nybyggerhistorie fra Spring Grove og omegn, Minnesota.* [Spring Grove, Minn.], Forfatterens Forlag, 1920.

Lovoll, Odd S. "*Decorah-Posten:* The Story of an Immigrant Newspaper." *Norwegian-American Studies* 27.77-101 (1977).

Luebke, Frederick C. "Legal Restrictions on Foreign Languages in the Great Plains States, 1917—1923." *Languages in Conflict: Linguistic Acculturation on the Great Plains,* ed. by Paul Schach (Lincoln, Neb.: University of Nebraska Press, 1980), 1—19.

Nartey, Jonas N.A. "Code-switching, Interference or Faddism? Language Use among Educated Ghanaians." *Anthropological Linguistics* 24.183—192 (1982)

Nelson, David T. *Luther College 1861—1961.* Decorah, Iowa: Luther College Press, 1961.

Venås, Kjell. *Hallingmålet.* Oslo: Det norske Samlaget, 1977.

5 Angående Luther College jfr. David T. Nelson, *Luther College* (1961).

6 Jfr. Haugen 1953 for en fullstendig beskrivelse av den norske innvandrers språk, særlig i midtvestens landbruksområder.

7 Se Haugen 1966 om den norske språkstrid.

8 Lovoll, s. 98; Haugen 1953, s. 148-9.

9 Jfr. Haugen 1953, s. 614 for mitt generelle inntrykk av Spring Grove som jeg undersøkte i 1942.

10 Jfr. O.S. Johnson, s. 15 og 118 om Rosendahls familiebakgrunn.

11 Jfr. Kjell Venås, *Hallingmålet* (1977) angående Hallingdialekten. Det ser ikke ut til at det finnes noen monografi om Hadelandsdialekten, men jeg er takknemlig for opplysninger jeg har fått fra Norsk Målførearkiv, Oslo. Jeg vil benytte anledningen til å takke Oskar Holter, Lysaker, som gav meg opplysningene.

12 Informasjon fra Oskar Petter Jensrud, Harestua, Norge. Iver Lynne ble født 1885. Han emigrerte i 1908 og kom tilbake i 1928. Han var siden kjent som «Iver Amerikaner».

13 Pers neste bemerkning får oss til å tvile på Lars' intellektuelle evner: han «gik sju aar for presten», dvs. det tok syv år før presten ville konfirmere ham. Vanligvis tok det da ett år (100).

14 De få gangene vi møter Olas kone er det tydelig at hun snakker samme dialekt som ham (Halling). Nedtrappingen av hennes rolle er en av de uforklarlige sidene ved tegneserien. Hun kommer tilbake fra Norge (160), så forlater hun ham og drar til Minneapolis (231), så kommer hun tilbake igjen (542), for snart å reise til Norge igjen (584).

15 Noen tilfeldige personer snakker trøndersk, f.eks. en kvinne ved Pers skistevne (173): *Æ trur æ gaar heim* og to fiskere som kutter is på Lake Superior: *Hi* (ha); *fingrain* (fingrene); *kain* (kan) (211). Kanskje var det vinterlandskapet som gjorde at han her valgte trøndersk. Det var ellers trøndere på Waterloo Ridge da jeg besøkte området.

16 Språkveksling er et emne som har vakt stor interesse blant forskere i tospråklighet i det senere: Jfr. J. Nartey 1982 og i henvisningene der. Se også Haugen 1953, s. 65, der fenomenet først ble benevnt og beskrevet.

17 Jfr. Haugen 1953, særlig sidene 255-260 når det gjelder virkningene på norsken. Jfr. Luebke 1980 for Midtvesten mer generelt.

18 Jfr. eksempler og diskusjon i Haugen 1953, s. 58-60.

19 Den tradisjonelle stavemåten *whiffletree* (jfr. Webster's *New International Dictionary* osv.) tar ikke tilstrekkelig hensyn til den vanlige uttalen i Midtvesten med *pp*. Den er kanskje oppstått ved tilknytning til ordet *whip* 'piske'.

20 Denne anekdoten forekommer også i O.S. Johnson, *Nybyggerhistorie,* s. 135 i beretningen om en ikke navngitt drukkenbolt. «Han hørte det lød kluk, kluk og da utbrøt han: 'Ja, jeg hører nok din røst, kjære vennen min, men jeg kan slet ikke hjælpe dig.'» Rosendahl kan ha lånt den fra Johnson, ettersom tegningen kom 14. mars 1924, fire år etter boken; eller det kan ha vært slikt som var på folkemunne 'i nabolaget'. Johnson skriver meget om drikking i Spring Grove.

21 Jfr. Haugen 1953, kapittel 16, når det gjelder lånordenes fonologi.

22 Her er det ikke brukt fagspråk. For detaljer se henvisningen i foregående note.

23 Jfr. Haugen 1953, kapittel 17, om lånordenes morfologiske tilpasning.

24 Jfr. Haugen 1953, kapittel 18, om dannelse av nye ord ved hjelp av lånord.

25 Statistikk i Haugen 1953, s. 265-67, fra årlige kirkerapporter.

1. Sagkyndig Hjælp tilkaldes.

2. Pær paa Veien til Naftedet.

3. "Bufineffen" begynder.

1. Competent help is summoned. "Hello — Is that you, Per? — Yes — And you're not in bed yet? — Fine weather — Yeah — Well, it'll probably rain — Oh no — So — Oh my — Yeah, you bet — Lemme see, are you busy tomorrow? — Well, I've got this new car — You couldn't help me start it up, I suppose? — That's just fine, Per — All right — Good bye!"

2. Per on his way to the scene.

3. The "business" begins. "One two three GO!"

4. Der ligger'n med Beina i Være.

5. Det Spinet vil inte lystre.

6. Hvor kunde nu ogsaa Ola vite det?

4. There he lies with his legs in the air. "Ola! Ola! Not so fast."

5. That beast won't obey. "Whoa Bill! Whoa Bill!" "Gee whiz!"

6. Now how could Ola know that? "Ola! Ola! Are you crazy? Where are you going?" "Keep still! Do I know where I'm going?"

---

kars (car) — bil
hello — hallo
ju bet (you bet) — javisst

aalreit (all right) — fint
godbai (goodbye) — farvel, adjø
business — forretning

one two three, go! — en to tre – gå!
ho (whoa) — ptro
gee whiz — jøssenam

(Tegninger for "Decorah-Posten" af Peter J. Rosendahl, Spring Grove, Minn.)

7. "Saiklon"-Kjælber god at ha.

7. A cyclone cellar is a good thing to have. "There comes a cyclone." "Run fast, grandpa."

8. Simpel Kunst at faa den paa ret Kjøl.

8. No trick to get it back on the right keel. "Shall I turn on the switch, Per?" "No, no! Just turn the throttle a little, then I'll swing it back on its feet again."

9 Det "biter" Grisen au.

9. This beats everything.

10. De kjører "paa hai".

10. They drive in high. "You could have got out of the road, you fool!" "We're driving in high, Halvor." "Ow, ow, ow! Ola, that hurt!" "It'll be another story when I get my mitts on you."

saiklon (cyclone) — syklon, hvirvelvind	svitsen (the switch) — bryteren trateln (the throttle) — bensinspjeldet	biter (beats) — overgår (alt) på hai (in high) — på høygir

1. "Can this really be true? It says they give five dollars for a skunk hide. I think we'd better start trapping skunks, Ola." "Yeah, you bet, let's do that. I'm with you, old boy."

All the good news appears in *Decorah-Posten*.

2. As the two neighbors start their hunting expedition, they see in their imagination rich rewards for their labors.

3. "It would be strange if there isn't a skunk up in that nice, big basswood oak here." "You're not as dumb as you look, Per, but let's keep going."

Per peers expectantly upwards, looking for the noble animal, which as everybody knows loves to climb trees.

4. After thorough study and lots of head scratching, they set up traps according to all the rules of the art.

5. "Hey, fellow! We've got an awful big one. I can just see his tail. But how are we going to kill him off?" "Lemme see, lemme see —Yes, here it says, page 925: 'Hit him on the neck with a stick.' In Norwegian that means 'Du ska gi'n eit drag over nakjin me ein stek.'"

Towards morning they find that their fondest hopes have been realized. But new problems arise.

6. "Now I'll pull him out, and at the same time I'll shout 'Go ahead,' and then you strike."

The Guide, however, gives answers to all questions, and Ola puts himself in a position to deal a well-directed blow.

7. "Go ahead!"

And as he goes "ahead" and whams the booty with all his might, the two "trappers" learn once more the truth of the old saw that "the last will be worse than the first." Afterwards they agree that they will write to *Decorah-Posten* and ask what kind of fool is putting such misleading news items in the paper.

---

skaankeskin — stinkdyrskinn
treppe — fange
skaank — stinkdyr
ju bet — fint

I am wid ju old boy — jeg blir med, gamle venn.
basvodeika — lindetreet

page — side
stek — stikke
gaa hed — kjør ivei
Guide — instruksjonsbok

Ver venlig mod Dyrene sier'n Ola!

1. "It grieves me to see how mean you are to the animals. They don't have anyone else's company to enjoy. You ought to be happy and — "

The tenderhearted Ola witnesses in horror and sadness the harsh treatment that Per shows to the dumb beasts and his indifference to their finer feelings.

2. " — grateful."

And — as we might expect — who appreciates Ola's magnanimity and is filled with gratitude is the cow.

3. "You needn't think you can make a fool of me, you old pig-head."

And there she sits, pouring out her salty tears in honor of the day, as she gets further instruction in humane education.

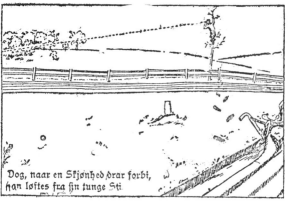

1. "Whoa, Jack! Whoa, Jill!"

A lonely working man, poor Per,
For him we have to shed a tear.

2. "'Tis sad indeed to wander
Alone upon this earth . . .'"

Hard it is to walk alone
And brood on thoughts that make one groan.

3. But when a beauty passes by,
He's raised above his grief so high.

4. And quickly he makes up his mind:
He'll ask and see if she is kind.

5. In gala dress, courageously,
He starts away, the girl to see.

6. "I see thee through the window,
Dear sweetest love of mine."

"My goodness! I wonder if she's thinking of me?"

From maiden's bower high aloft
He hears her humming love songs soft.

7. "Sjur, Sjur! Goodness me — uff —
here comes — uff — a uff — oh dear, ow,
ow — "

"Here, Watch, here Watch, come, Watch!"

In a one-two-three he briskly climbs
The ladder with his stiff old limbs.

8. "I never saw the like of this before."
"No, nor I either — you miserable fool."
"Here Watch, here Watch, sick 'em Watch."

But by a nasty trick of fate
He never found his hoped-for mate.

9. "It would have been better if I had stayed home. These womenfolk are just a bunch of good-for-nothing tramps anyway." "Sick 'em, sick 'em there, sick 'em, Watch!"

And pappa ne'er could understand
The purpose of this courting man.

When beauty now in after days
Appears on his unhappy ways,
He slyly laughs at all his pain:
"I'll never go through that again."

Vatch — navn på buhunden
siggem — ta'n

Per tilkalder Hjælp.

Hvordan de "fixer" 'a.

1. Per calls for help. "Hello, Ola. You've gotta come pretty quick and help me put a ring on the snout of this big sow. God help me if she isn't rooting up everything, whether it's loose or fast. The nasty swine. Goodbye."

2. How they fix her. "You hang on to her tail, Ola, and then I'll soon fix her, man." "I'll hold her by the tail, you just go ahead."

Og hvordan Purka fixer dem.

3. And how the sow fixes them.

fixer — ordne med, fikser   gaa hed — driv på
hello — hallo
purty quick — temmelig fort
godbai — lev vel

1. "You must be sure you get blood so we can make *klubb* (black pudding, blood pudding)." "Well, I think we're ready to start." "Yes, mam."

2. "All ready." "Here it goes."

4. "You had no business sticking your bean in there — you miserable idiot."

starte — begynne
yes mam — ja frue
aal reddi — helt ferdig

hadde ingen bisnes te aa — hadde ikke noe med å

1. "What'll we do with the hide, Per."
"We'll have to send it up to Minneapolis."

(Dynamite)

2. "Hurry up! Hurry up! Hear how he's growling!"

4. "Who's making all this infernal racket?"

5. "By thunder!"

hurry op — skynd deg   *bai tønder* — fanken au

"Paa Ridestellet skal Storfolk kjendes," sa Ola til Kjäringen om Ford'en hendes.

8

"Big Shots Are Known by Their Riding Gear," Said Ola to His Wife about Her Ford.*

(Dedicated to our Subscribers in Houston County, Minnesota)

* Ironic quotation from Ibsen's *Peer Gynt.*

1. "Are you off on a big trip today, Ola?"
"Oh no, we're just going over to Waterloo
Ridge for a Ladies Aid party."

2. "Ola! Ola! You lost the back wheels.
Put on the brake — "

3. "How can I make the brake hold, silly,
when the wheels are gone! I'll try turning
around Wilmington and then I'll come
back the other way."

4. "I'll fasten this rope to the radiator cap
and then I'll jump out and hang on to it."

5. "Whoa back!"

---

brekken — bremsen, brekken
Waterloo Ridge (i Houston County,
Minnesota)

Wilmington — by i staten Minnesota
redietorkæppen — radiatorlokket
ho back — ptro (til hest)

1. "I can't understand why such a fine fellow as I am never has any luck with the girls."

2. "Well, the thing is that you can't talk Yankee, Per."

3. "But what do I say when I meet a girl on the sidewalk then?"
   "You tip your hat and say, 'Hello, pie face!'"

4. "Hello, pie face!"

5. "'How can you forget old Norway?'"*

* Popular Norwegian-American song.

yeinki — amerikansk (engelsk)   *hello* — hallo
seidvaaken — fortauget   *pie face* — paifjes

1. "It's peculiar that you can never learn to split wood, Per!"

2. "You'd better teach me then, since you're so smart!"

3. "You place the log on its end. Then you sink the axe firmly into it — " "Yes!"

4. " — and lift it up with full speed — " "Yes!"

5. " — and smack it down with all your strength." "Ye — "

splitte — kløve, spalte
yas — ja
spid — fart

1. "Hello, Per! You're working in the potato field?" "Oh hello! Yeh, I'm doin' that." "Well, I would like to know if you could board the teacher this winter?" "No, I can't board fellows like that. They're so particular — "

2. "This winter it's not a man who's going to teach. It's a young girl from Minneapolis." "— But if she'll be satisfied with my poor offerings, I'll do the best I can."

3. "Well, now I'll have to hurry to the depot and pick her up. The pudding will be just the right temperature to eat when we get back. I was lucky to get plenty of butter."

4. (Norw. tr.:) "Og er rommet mitt utstyrt med damp-oppvarming, varmt og kaldt vann, og er det bad og elektrisk —." "Ja, ja, jeg tror det."

5. "Don't you suppose that black rascal has eaten up the sausage!"

---

borde — holde med kosten, ha i pensjon
teacher'n — læreren

potetfili — potetåkeren
depon — jernbanestasjonen
ay tank so — jeg tror det

1. "Hello, Per! Yes, and you too — So you're fine over there? — How's it going with you and the teacher? Ha! Ha! Ha! Oh, I thought I'd start up tomorrow if it's all right with you. Well, goodbye now."

2. "I can't understand what this knob is for." "Oh shucks! I'll show you that."

3. "It's no trick to run such a thing. Just give the horse a lash, Ola. My goodness, this —" "Giddap, Frank!"

4. "— makes the manure so fine —" "Giddap, giddap!"

En brydsom Kalv — og en uventet Modtagelse.   A Troublesome Calf — and an Unexpected Reception   13

1. "Now get out of here again!"

2. "Are you back still once more?"

3. "Come on!"

4. "Now you're coming for the last time!"

shucks — pokkern
trik — kunst
ge dep — hypp
kom an — bare kom

1. "Even if the sidewalk was half a forty wide, I guess it would still be too narrow."

2. "I'm wondering if I can't put something over on them anyway." "If you can do that, Per, then you are smart."

3. (Norw. tr.) "Hei, jenter! La dere merke til Maries nye flamme på kinoen i går kveld?" "Ja, er ikke det en fin kar?" "Han er toppen!" "Å men er ikke han en stor sjarmør!"

Det er aldrig saa galt at det ikke kunde gaaet værre. Things Are Never So Bad They Couldn't Be Worse 15

1. "I'm afraid you can't handle it, Per." "I'll have to tie the hayfork rope to it, for safety's sake, so it won't go too far if I lose control of it."

2. "Oh boy! It's making at least a mile an hour — maybe even two."

4. "I wasn't so dumb after all when I tied it to the oak. If I hadn't done so, things might have gone absolutely wrong."

---

seidvaaka —fortauget
førtivæg — førti acres' vei, bredden av et jordstykke på 40 acres, dvs. ca. 160 mål.

handle — styre
lose control — miste kontroll
mila — 1,6 km. (amerikansk mil)

Da Fortjenesten sprang i Luften.

1. "That's a strange machine you have here, but what are you going to use it for?" "My oh my how little you know, Ola. That's one of these force feeders to feed pigs with. I'll start it up and give a demonstration."

2. "It's a simple matter to fatten up a pig when you have a machine like this. Imagine, I shipped three pigs to Equity the other day. They tipped the scale at fifteen hundred pounds." "That certainly is a strange device."

3. "No, I've never heard of anything like this." "Well sir, this fall I'm going to ship pigs for many thousands of dollars. I'll tell you there's money in the pig business. It's a business that never blows up, so to speak —"

Eika brast og hele Stasen gik i Vasken. The Oak Broke and the Whole Business Went Down the Drain 17

1. "Hey, Per! Come, let's go fishing."

2. "Boy, this is really going to be a picnic. Just see how they're jumping." "Yeah, you bet."

3. "Now I've got a real whopper." "I've got one, too."

force feeder — tvangsforingsmas-
    kin
feede — fore
shippa — sendte (til marked)

equity — kooperative
pund — (0,4 kilo)

picnic — fest, moro
ju bet — det er sikkert

1. "I think I have enough to top it with." "Yes, that'll be just right."

2. "Does it look pretty good? Maybe you'll go and get the ladder, Ola." "It looks as if I had set it up myself."

3. "I'm coming right away." "Oh, there's no hurry."

4. "You don't need to bring the ladder, Ola. I think I made it down all right."

1. "I s'pose I'll have to try and fix this good-for-nothing blower again. Ola and the crew will probably come dragging in sometime today."

2. "We'd better start up this sod, anyway, I think. Per is always so slow getting up in the morning."

3. "It's all clogged up, man." "Doesn't it turn over?" "I think the belt's slipping." "Maybe the gears are stripped." "Oh no, it's jumping the cog."

4. "What's bothering you now again?"

töppe — sette topp på	*blower'n* — blåsemaskina	*belte* — reima	*jompa* — hoppa
	crewa — arbeidsgjengen	*slippa* — glir, glipper	*cog* — tann (på hjulet)
	soden — torva	*gear'n* — giret, tannhjulet	*badra* — plager
	upclogga — tiltettet	*strippa* — ødelagt, nedslitt	

Lars finder ud hvad "slo" betyder i Amerika.

1. "Where are you going, Per?" "To the depot to meet my brother Lars who's coming from Norway."

2. "Well, hello, Lars." "Well, hello, Per."

3. "Do you always drive at this speed, Per?" "Oh no, I seldom drive as slow as this."

4. "Oh dear, don't drive so fast!" "This isn't any speed at all."

5. "Didn't your brother Lars come today?" "Sure, he — Well, did you ever! I think I must have lost that son-of-a-gun on the way."

Per kommer i en slem Knibe.

1. "Do you know what I've been thinking about, Per? Let's go over to Sjur's woods and pick butternuts; he won't mind that." "I'll go with you; you can depend on that."

2. "Are there any butternuts up in this oak?" "Yes, you bet — there are lots of them."

3. "Look out, Per! There comes Sjur."

---

depon — stasjonen
butternuts — smørvalnøtter
depende paa — *lite på*
slo — langsomt

ja ju bet — ja visst
speed — fart
son-ov-a-gun — fordømte tullingen

1. "By jiminy!"

2. "Hey, Ola! Come here. I have a big log I can't manage to lift."

3. "I can manage to lift it all right."

4. "Haw haw haw, ho ho ho ho, oh my, oh my, oh ho, ha ha —"

En uventet Medhjælper.

An Unexpected Helper   23

1. "We ought to have cleaned this well before we went away." "Yes, but we didn't have time then."

2. "Do you remember how deep it is?" "It's eleven and eighty feet down to the water level."

3. "You better hang on tight to the rope. There's probably more water here." "When I hold on to the rope, Ola, you're perfectly safe."

---

bai jiminy — herre gud
fot — ca. 30 cm
log — tømmerstokk

vaterlevel'n — vannstanden
cleana — renset opp
safe — trygg

2. "You don't really understand this kind of thing, Ola. Let me do it, who knows how." "Is that so?"

3. "First I generally walk a little forward and then a little backward, and then again — look, look! Now it twists itself. I'm not far away from water —"

4. "— I'm sure of that." "No, I think that's right."

Per skiller sig af med en kjær Ven.

Per Takes His Leave of a Dear Friend 25

1. "It kind of hurts to sell this old sow. But I have to do it now that she's so fine and fat." "Oh, you'll forget it soon, Per. I always feel this way too when I sell my pigs."

2. "There comes the teacher." "Woof!"

3. "Whoa!" "Whoa!"

4. "Do you have any idea just what it was that happened, Per?" "Wait a little, Ola, until I can gather my thoughts together again."

feela — føler
teachern — læreren
ho — ptro
hæpna — hendte

1. "After lunch we'll go off with the sow, Ola. She's gotta come with us this time." "If only we can get her up in the truck, we're saved."

2. "Do you remember, Per, the old days when we drove our pigs to town in the lumber wagon?" " Yes indeed, Ola, you can be sure I remember. It's remarkable how everything has changed."

3. "Did you ever see such a nosy pig!"

4. "Woof!"

Per gaar paa frieriod.

1. "Per, have you seen the new hired girl at the Johnsons'? She's a real humdinger. If I were in your shoes, I'd go over and call on her." "Is that the truth you're telling me, Ola?"

2. "Tra la la la la la." " Oh thou beautiful, delightful butterfly."

3. "S-sh, Marit! There's a tramp behind the snowball bush there."

4. "Get out of here, you good-for-nothing hobo!"

---

trøkken — lastebilen
hyrejenta — tausa
snøballbuska — snøballtreet
  (viburnum)

lombervøgni — lastevogna
kaale — hilse på
chænga — forandra seg
træmp — fant, lasaron

1. "Confound it anyway — we forgot the whippletree." "Oh say, Lars, will you go get the whippletree?"

2. "The whippletree? The whippletree?"

3. "The whippletree?"

4. "I just wonder if this isn't one of those whippletrees?"

Per "retter Smed for Bager", eller Kua som fik undgjælde for Grisen.

1. "Are you going to shoot rabbits, Per?" "No! I'm going to shoot this stupid sow."

2. "Now you can whistle, you swine!"

3. "Uff."

---

*Caption: *Allusion to poem by Johan Herman Wessel, "Smeden og Bageren"*
say — hør*

hyppeltræe — svingel, tverrtre (som fester selene sammen på et hestepar)

1. "Are you looking for something, Per?" "I have to try and kill some of all these rats, you see."

2. "Ow, ow, Ola! I have a rat in my pants."

3. "Here she sits." "Take away your hand."

Per er aldrig hjælpeløs.

Per Is Never at a Loss 31

2. "We've smashed the wheel all to pieces. We'll never get to the picnic this way!" "Oh dear, oh dear."

3. "I know what we'll do, Ola. Let me go along beside the fender and support the axle."

4. "Am I driving too fast maybe?" "Oh, never y' mind!"

---

kille — slå i hjel
smæsja — knust
picnic'n — utflukten

fender'n — skjermbrettet
never y' mein' — aldri bry deg

Et probat Middel mod Bog-Agenter.

1. "Your pigs are great, Per." "I don't care what they are. I wish I never had to see a pig again. Here I have to work like a slave and wade in the manure year in and year out —"

2. "— Never have I had a happy day, and I'll never get one either. They say it's so wonderful to live on the farm — yeah, you bet! I'll sell bag and baggage and move to town —" "There comes a book agent, Per."

3. "Hello boys! It's fine weather. Well sirree, this is a fine farm and fine buildings and a bunch of wonderfully handsome pigs. It must be delightful to live here. I have a book here —". "Uh huh."

4. "I've heard that song before, but let's get another verse anyhow. Here ye are." "Oh golly, man! Oh Per, oh Per!"

Per gir Bul'n en Lærepenge.

1. "So help us, there comes that strange, angry bull."

2. "It's a good thing this turned out as it did, Ola." "We had good luck, Per, so far, but it'll be tough hanging here in this cold wind."

3. "I'll try pouring on him this kerosene I have in my jug here. Then you can light a match and drop it down." "Well, we can always try it and see if it has any effect."

4. "I'll bet he's going up that hill in high, man."

---

farmen — bondegården	*anyhow* — lell	*taaf* — stridt	*paa hai* — i høygir
hello boys — goddag gutter	*her' ye are* — her har du det	*kerosin* — parafin	
well sørri — ja visst	*golly* — jøsses	*jaaggen* — krukka, dunken	
bunch — flokk	*bull* — okse, stut	*bette* — vedde	

1. "I wonder what's happened to Per to-day."

2. "Ola hasn't come yet today, I see."

3. "Oh my! It's awful hot today."

1. "Why, are you sick, Per?" "Uh-huh! toothache." "I'll cure that in a hurry."

2. "But won't it hurt?" "Not at all. This will go so fast that the tooth will be out before you know it. These dentists don't know everything either, I tell you, Per."

3. "I'm afraid this is going to hurt any-way." "Pull the wire up tight, Per. Now I'll give it a blow."

uhu — ja-a
kure — kurere
dentistadn — tannlegene

wiren — ståltråden, vaiern
teit — stramt

Per og Ola paa Vei til Statefæra.

1. "If you feel as I do, Per, we'll go to the fair in St. Paul." "Yes, I'll go with you."

2. "But what shall I do when I get to University Avenue then?" " What you shall do? All you have to do is to keep close behind me all the way."

3. "Is that the road to St. Paul?" "Yes sir, straight ahead." [Sign:] "Slow down, sharp turn."

4. "What are you doing here, you fool?" "Didn't you say I should keep close behind you?"

Per "fixer" Høiforken.

1. "Whoa! Whoa! Stop, Per. Something has caught. Will you climb up and look?"

2. "It's nothing but this knob here that has slipped. Tighten up the rope a little."

3. "About like that?"

4. "Now the fork lets go real well, Per."

statefæra — statsutstillinga (for Minnesota)
fairn — utstillinga, fesjået
University Avenu' — gate i St. Paul og Minneapolis (Universitetsgata)
keepe klos — holde deg nær
Is dat de raad to St. Paul? — Er det veien til S. P.?
Yes sir straight ahead — Ja da, rett fram
ho — ptro
kætja — hengt seg fast
nabben — knaggen
slippa — glidd av
forken — (høy)gaffelen
Skiltet i 36.3: Sakte fart, skarp sving

Et uventet Besøg — Per drar tilskogs.

1. "Ola, tell me what you think about this new night shirt I've gotten from Sears, Roebuck Co." "Well, it wouldn't have hurt if it had been a size larger."

2. "Ssh! Somebody's knocking at the door. Go and see who it is." "A book agent, I suppose."

3. "It's the minister's wife!"

Per og Ola faar en "Surpris".

1. "How do you feel after you got back home again, Per?" "Oh, I feel extra good."

2. "But there are a lot of things to fix up, I'll tell you." "Yes, I suppose there are."

3. "One thing I'm grateful for is that the old sow hasn't showed up again." "I don't wonder at that, Per."

Sears, Roebuck Co. — velkjent postordrefirma
ein size — et nummer

fila — føler (du) deg
fixe paa — rette på
showa op — vist seg

1. "Are you making a Turkish bath, Per?" "Oh no. I'm just going to dip my calves. Confound it if they aren't so lousy it's a dirty shame." [Stock dip]

2. "Watch out, Ola, so it doesn't splash in your eyes."

3. "Watch out for yourself, Per."

4. "Do you think it did any good?" "Pfui!"

1. "Lars, maybe you'll plow the corn today? Ola and I have to go around and get signers on a road petition." "Yes, I'll be glad to." "But be careful when you hitch up, Lars."

2. "Well, now I guess everything is right. But then it's a question of getting some life into these lazy horses."

3. "Giddap!"

5. "If anyone should ask me, I'd have to answer that here in America one does not get treated in the way I had expected."

---

dippe — dyppe
stock dip — desinfiserende veske til buskapen
kaunne — maisen

seinera — undertegnere
raad potesjen — veisøknad
hitcher opp — spenner for
ge dæp — hypp, hypp

1. "It's awful how tight this saw is." "Yeah, I think so too."

2. "I'll pull the end down, so you can try sawing by yourself." "Yeah sure."

3. "Is it working better now, Ola?" "You bet."

4. "Now you can let go, Per."

1. "If the horses run too fast, Lars, you'll have to hold the reins very tight." "Oh, I'll manage it all right." "I'll crank up, Ola."

2. "Giddap!"

3. " Whoa! Whoa!"

4. "Hold the reins tight!" " I'm holding all I can."

---

teit — trangt, trått
ja shure — ja visst
ju bet — det er sikkert
krænker opp — sveiver opp motoren

ge dæp — hypp hypp
ho — ptro

3. "Ha ha ha. That was just what Ola had coming to him. He didn't need to walk around with his nose so up in the air. Ha ha ha."

4. "Ha ha ha!"

1. " Your bell cow is in your corn field, Per."

3. "Sick 'em there." "Moo-oo-oo —"

4. "You're gonna remember this trip a while, I think." "Yes, and I too." "Moo-oo-oo —"

kønfila — maisåkeren
sik em — ta'n

1. "It'll be tough to hang up there and fix something like that." "Yea, and still tougher to tip it over when we don't have anything to do it with."

2. "Maybe you can think up a plan, Per, you've got such brains." "Lemme see —, lemme see—."

3. "I got it, Ola! We'll dig some of the dirt away, so it'll settle down sufficiently for us to reach it." "Oh my, Per!!"

4. One month later.

5. "Right, now we've got her ready." "Just about."

Per og Ola "tester" Brua.

Per and Ola "Test" the Bridge   47

1. "Oh say, Per — I got a telegram today from headquarters that we have to inspect this new bridge right away and send in a report. Hurry up and come with me."

2. "Do you have the blanks and the instruments with you, Per?" "Yeah, sure."

3. "Now Ola, listen here! You drive the test load slowly across the bridge while I go down below and note the result. You get me?" "I think so."

4. "Is that far enough, Per?" "Stop, stop, not so fast!"

---

taaf — vanskelig	settler ned — synker på plass	hedkvarters — hovedkvarteret,	hørri up — skynd deg	yu get me — forstår du meg?
fixe — reparere	sufesjent — tilstrekkelig	myndighetene	blanksadn — skjemaene	ay tank so — jeg tror det
le' me see — få sjå	rikjer opp — nå opp	inspekte — inspisere	sjur — sjølsagt	
digge — grave	jost about — så omtrent	reit ævei — straks	test lode — prøvelasset	

1. "How about it, Lars, can you go to the mill and get the feed? You see, I and Ola have to be on the jury today." "But look out, Lars, when you harness Kate. She's a bit nervous when you put the crupper on."

2. "Ola's a gifted man, but perhaps I'm not so stupid either. Whoa, Kate!"

3. "Whoa! Whoa, Kate!"

4. "Whoa! Whoa!"

5. "Whoa there!"

6. "Whoa back!"

Lars og "Potet Buggen".

Lars and the Potato Bugs   49

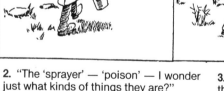

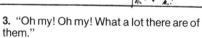

1. "Well, what shall I do today?" "Suppose you start killing potato bugs. I'll fix up the sprayer for you and mix up some poison." "Lemme see —"

2. "The 'sprayer' — 'poison' — I wonder just what kinds of things they are?"

3. "Oh my! Oh my! What a lot there are of them."

4. "Oh dear!"

5. "How glorious is my land of birth, Bewreathed with seas around its earth." [Norwegian patriotic song]

---

fid'n — fôret
crupper'n — bakreima
ho — ptro!

suppose — hva om
kille — slå i hjel, drepe
sprayer'n — sprøyten

peisen — gift
potetbuggen — potetbillen

1. "There's a salesman here who wants to talk to you, Per."

2. "Are there still any of those rascals around here?"

3. "Darn if I won't beat up on 'im —"

4. — by thunder!"

5. "Why hello! I am pleased to meet you." "Please meet, yas."

1. "You want to go with me to a surprise party, Ola?" "Yeah sure, if you'll wait till I get my butter made."

2. "So your wife isn't home?" "No, she left for Norway last spring."

3. "How does she enjoy it over there?" "I haven't heard from her."

4. "I'll be done in a minute, Per."

---

bai tønder — for fanken
Why hello! I am pleased to meet you — God dag, så hyggelig å treffe deg.

surpreisparti — selskap til overraskelse for hedersgjesten
sjur — sjølsagt

Per og Ola paa Bjørnejagt.

1. "Per! Per! Come with your gun!"

2. "Just what's the matter?" "Oh — oh — a bear — ha — uff — took the cow —"

3. "Don't worry, Ola. I'll bring that fellow home all right."

4. "Here I come with him."

Ola "kurerer" Hesten hans Per.

1. "Oh, would you please come home with me, Ola. I have a sick horse."

2. "It's easy enough to cure him. All you have to do is to thump him on the skull." "Thump him on the skull, what exactly is that?" "I'll soon show you."

3. "Now take your sledgehammer, Per, and strike the plank. That'll give a jar that will quicken up his nerves." "You don't say!"

4. "That's right."

dont wørri — aldri bry deg du
kure — kurere
jar — støt,

kvikner opp — stimulerer
nervsa — nervene
dats reit — det er riktig

1. "Oh, would you come here, Per. I've got an aspen poplar hung up here."

2. "I don't understand how I'm going to get it down." "Goodness, how little you know."

3. "Watch close how I do it now, and then you'll know for another time." "I'm watching as hard as I can."

4. "Gee whiz! There it fell."

"Kaunting" som Middel mod Søvnløshed.

Counting As a Remedy for Insomnia   55

1. "Don't you feel well today, Per? ARE YOU SICK, Per? PER?" No answer.

2. "Do you have it in your stomach or in your head?" "I can't sleep at night."

3. "I know the remedy for that, too, Per. When you've gone to bed tonight, you start counting the clock ticks, and before you know it, you'll sleep like a log."

4. "One, two, three, four — "

5. Next morning

6. "— ninetyfive thousand, three hundred and six — ninetyfive thousand three hundred and seven — ninetyfive —"

---

gudnes — du verden
vatch klos — pass nøye på

fila — føle seg
te bed — til sengs
starter — begynner
kaunte — telle

Per prøver de nye "Styregreier".

1. "I wondered if you could drive the superintendent, Per. You see I'm bound to go to St. Paul to a convention."

2. "But is this self-steering outfit any good?" "You bet! It's extra. All you have to tend to is the throttle and the spark."

3. "I s'pose you are used to driving a car —" "Yas, yas, ay dreiv purti kvik."

4. "Oh mercy, let me off!"

5. "Ay tank vi bot get off."

Paa Jagt efter "Moonshiners".

1. "Look here, Ola, I got an order to clean up a nest of moonshiners in the north part of the county. What do you think of that?" "Gee whiz!"

3. "Sh — sh."

4. "But how can we find out if it's moonshine?" "Oh, I guess we'd better taste it."

5. "Yes indeed, this is moonshine." "Same over here."

6. "Yes, we love this land of ours."[National anthem of Norway]

---

superintenten — skolesjefen
baund — nødt
konvensjen — møte
denna self stearing outfit'n —

denne sjølstyrende greia
ju bet — ja visst
tende — passe på
trattel'n — bensinspjeldet

order — ordre
kline opp — rense opp
nest — reir
munsheiners — heimebrennere

kaunti — fylke
gee whiz — du all verden
munshein — heimebrent
same overhare — likeså her

The Engine is "missing".

1. "I don't like it, Ola, that they have to run our pictures in *Decorah Posten* all the time." "No, I don't either. Let's go down there and order them to stop it."

2. "You know, Per, that I haven't seen Decorah since I went to the Breckinridge school." "Well sir, I guess I have only been there once, too."

3. "Isn't it great stuff how they've fixed up the road here?" "Yeah, you bet."

4. "Say boys — your engine is missing."

5. "What did he say, Ola?" "He said that we had lost our engine."

6. "I'll bet that it fell out when we drove over that stone in the Big Canoe Hill." "I suspected that at once. We're bound to find it again."

Per er en "Klypper" til at koge Graut.

1. "Wait a while, Ola, and you'll get supper before you leave — The *graut* (porridge, pudding) will be ready soon." "Oh, you mustn't bother, Per."

2. "All this fancy food they use nowadays — I can't bear it. I'll take *graut* every time." "You're a real whiz at making *graut*, Per."

3. "I don't feel good, Per." "Neither do I — it sort of burns in my chest."

4. "Well, this beats everything! I made a mistake and used some of the plaster of paris I had in a basin here."

---

rønne — trykke
ordre — beordre, befale
Brækenrig — sted nær Decorah
vel sør — nå ja
fixa — stelt
raad'n — vegen
ju bet — ja visst

(Forbipasserende:) "Hei, gutter, motoren tenner ikke riktig."
injeina — motoren
bette — vedde
Bekenu — sted nær Decorah
(Merk at "missing" også betyr at noe er borte)

suspekta — mistenkte
baund te — nødt til

supper — kveldsmat
badre — bry deg
fænsi — flotte
every teim — hver gang

fila — føler meg
bitar — overgår
plaster paris'n — murpussen
beise — balje, vaskefat

1. "But how can we hoist it up so that we get hold of the piston rings?" "Oh, I've provided for that all right."

2. "You're a clever fellow, Per, who can use a bucky mule for something like this." "Oh, I know a lot more tricks like that, Ola."

3. "It hurts me so deeply to see how they mistreat animals here in America."

4. "Poor animal — now you're free."

𝔇𝔞 𝔭𝔢𝔯 𝔬𝔤 𝔒𝔩𝔞 𝔰𝔨𝔲𝔩𝔡𝔢 𝔩𝔞𝔤𝔢 "𝔊𝔦𝔤𝔱𝔪𝔢𝔩𝔢𝔰𝔦𝔫".

When Per and Ola Were Going to Make Rheumatism Medicine 61

1. "Per, here it says you can make a medicine for rheumatism out of rattlesnake fat." "Did you ever hear the like! I saw a rattler on the south forty yesterday."

2. "Do you have enough nerve so that you dare catch it then?" "Oh sure."

3. "Poke into the shock with your stick, Ola, and then I'll catch it just as it comes out."
"Now you've gotta be quick, Per."

4. "S-r-r-r-" "Ow! Ow!"

---

piston ringan — stempelringene
proveida — sørga for
baakki — sta

mule — muldyr
triks — knep, tricks

rættelsnæk — klapperslange
førtin — et jordstykke på 40 acres
(= 120 mål)

nørv — mot
kætjen — fange den
sjakken — haugen med kornbånd

1. "How does it happen that you tie your-self down with a rope, Per?" "Well, I won't fall down then, you see, if I should lose my balance."

2. "Dear me, Per, don't be so careless." "Uff! I have such a pain in my back."

3. "Oh dear!"

1. "My, what's happened to you, Per?" "Oh, I just got hurt kicking a cow."

2. "I can't understand how you managed to do that." "Well, you see I got so awfully mad that I jumped up and —"

3. "— kicked with all my might exactly —"

4. "— like this!!" "Oh yas, ay see."

---

kærles — uforsiktig
safety first — omtrent = trygg tra- fikk

hæpna — hendt
aa yas, ay see — å ja, jeg ser det

Ola og Per laver en Molbohistorie.

1. "Have you made a cement cover on the cistern, too?" "Yes, and one that is solid, too."

2. "You can brick it up and fill in with dirt, and then I'll finish up inside." "Yes, I'll do that."

3. "Do you need me any more today, Per?" "No, you can stop when you're through with this, Ola."

4. "Are you there, Ola? Can't you answer? Ola! Ola!! OLA!!!"

Per ved Raad for Uraad.

1. "This is a real bad fix. Both the wheels are off. We have to phone to the garage and get help." "Yes, but they're so shamefully expensive."

2. "But what shall we do then, Per?" "Just wait a little, Ola, and I'll show you what we can do."

3. "Can you hold it up then?" "Oh sure, that's no trick at all."

4. "Is it tough, Per?" "Not at all, just keep driving, Ola."

---

cover — dekke, lokk
cistern — brønn
finishe — gjøre ferdig
inseid — på innsida

fone — ringe
itte no triks ætaal — slett ikke noe problem
taaf — hardt

1. "We ought to finish up the grubbing by noon if we have enough dynamite." "We have about fifty pounds, and I think that's plenty."

2. "My goodness, if that good-for-nothing sow isn't eating up the dynamite."

3. "Look out!" "Blast me, if I don't kill you dead!"

1. "Is that you, Per? There's fire in the barn here — come quick!"

3. "Hello, Per — do you want to go with us on a picnic?" "Yes, do, Per." "Oh goodness we'll have such fun." "Jump in, Per."

5. "You mustn't be bashful, Per." "I think I'll be eating myself to death. Hee hee, and I was supposed to help Ola with his fire, too. Hee, hee —"

---

finishe up — gjøre fra oss
grubbinga — stubbebrytinga
my gudnes — herregud
look out — pass deg

faiermand — brannmann
barn — fjøset
picnic — landtur, picnic
aa gudnes — du verden

jump in — hopp inn
feier'n — brannen

1. "I thought today we should try to hoist up again that windmill we dug down. Have you time to come along, Per?" "Yeah sure, I'm just going to the depot to get that Victrola I ordered."

2. "Giddap!" "One - two - three - GO!" "Giddap, Kate!"

3. "Whoa! Whoa! Stop Per, Kate has bucked."

4. "Giddap, giddap, Kate!" "Giddap!"

5. "Go on here!" "Giddap!" "Giddap!"

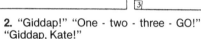

1. "There wasn't much use in my buying a run-about — they won't have anything to do with me anyway — nobody wants a ride —" "It's your own fault, Per. You're just too slow moving. You have to be quick, you see, and take them by surprise."

2. "By jiminy! There comes a girl who wants a ride."

3. "Hey you! Want a ride?"

5. "Well, a lot of good that did!"

---

digga — grov	*depon* — jernbanestasjonen	*rønnæbaut* — småbil	*bai jiminy* — hei san
ja sjur — ja sjølsagt	*victrolan* — grammofonen	*ride* — skyss	*want a ride* — vil du ha skyss
baakka — steilet	*ordra* — bestilte	*slo* — sein	
gedep — hypp hypp		*i motion* — i vendinga	

1. "Some fellow phoned me today and asked if we could split posts tomorrow over there by Nonpartisan Highway." "Oh, I suppose we can do that."

2. "Now, whack it with your axe, Per." "Here she goes!"

4. "I get so annoyed with you, Ola. You're always carrying on some kind of foolery. Now I got my axe spoiled, too."

1. "It's Per's birthday today, so we'd better make it a holiday. If it gets too tiresome, Lars, you can take a walk." "Oh, I'll figure something out."

2. "Ah, how charming it is to get out into nature's open air!"

3. "But what do we have here?"

4. "Just as I thought, a colony of these big flies —"

5. "Ha ha, now we'll get some action —"

---

fona — ringte
splitte post — hogge til gjerdestolper
highway — landevei

spår — vil jeg tro
hare she goes — her går det
fuleri — narreri
spøila — skjemt ut

walk — spasertur
et sørpræisparti — se nr. 51

1. "What's wrong now again?" "Lars fell into the well —"

2. "I can't understand how we're gonna get him up again." "Oh, sure, we'll fill it up with water, so he floats up."

3. "Can you catch sight of him?" "No, but I can hear 'im splashing."

4. "We don't need any more water, Per. I can reach him with the hook now."

5. "Now I've got hold of 'im."

6. "Are you feeling all right, Lars?" "Yes, thanks, but it was confoundedly wet."

1. "Come home with me, Ola, so you can see my new manure carrier." "Oh, have you got a new carrier?"

2. "Isn't it heavy pulling?" "No, it's nothing at all."

3. "But how can you get it emptied?" "I tip it over sidewise. Just wait a little, and you'll see."

5. "Ha ha ha!"

fila — føle seg
aalreit — bra

manur' carrier'n — møkk-kjærra
ætaal — i det hele tatt
tipper — velter

Denne Gang var det Kua, som gik i Heisen.

1. "Are you already going to milk, Per?" "Yes, I was anxious to try out my new milking stool."

2. "I'm so bothered by their going to pieces." "Well, this one ought to hold all right."

3. "Moo-o-o" "Per must be busy trying out his new stool."

4. "Did this stool go to pieces, too?" "Oh no. This time it was the cow that got smashed."

Da Lars skulde stelle hjemme.

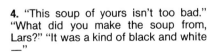

1. "You must have dinner ready when we come back Lars. You can make soup, potatoes, and pudding." "But what shall I make soup with when we don't have any meat?" "Take my gun, Lars, and shoot a rabbit or a partridge or something like that."

3. "I hope the soup tastes better than it smells."

4. "This soup of yours isn't too bad." "What did you make the soup from, Lars?" "It was a kind of black and white —"

5. "— here you can see the hide."

---

badra — plaget

patris — rapphøne, en slags rype
(Skinnet er av et stinkdyr, "skunk")

1. "Well, Lars, today you can either wash clothes or go grubbing." "Take your choice." "I prefer to wash clothes."

2. "Ouch! Ouch! Ouch! Help! Help! —"

3. "He's all in, man." "Let's lay 'im in the shade there."

4. "We have to pour some strong stuff into him." "There's nothing left in the big jug, Per. Take the one standing on the table."

1. "What does it say there, Ola?" "It says that we have to drive at least forty miles an hour down Main Street."

2. "And our speed was no more than five miles an hour. What shall we do now?" "We're bound to back up and try to get more speed."

3. "Now it's running 45 miles an hour."

4. "Keep it up, Ola."

---

grubbe — grave opp stubber
tæk yur choice — du har fritt valg
all in — helt utkjørt
jaaggen — krukka, dunken

Speed limit 40 miles per hour — Fartsgrense 40 miles (64 km) i timen
Main Street — hovedgata

spidn — farten
baund — nødt
bæke up — rygge
keep it op — kjør på

Lars "feeder" Kalvene.

1. "You'll have to milk, Lars, and feed the calves. Per's going to give the main speech at the chicken dinner, so we haven't the time to do it." "You can depend on me."

2. "Co — bossy, co — bossy!"

3. "Stop it, stop it!"

4. "Ow! Ow! Ow!"

Lars som Tømmerhugger.

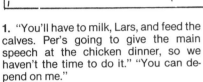

1. "I think we'd better get Lars to split that post that is left over there by the bridge." "Yes, we certainly don't have time to monkey with it."

2. "But be careful, Lars, so you don't get hurt." "Oh, I am a grown man after all."

---

feede — gi (mat), fôre
chicken dinner'n — festmiddag
   med kylling
hol' an — stå stille

posten — (her) tømmerstokken
monki — klusse
hørta — skadd

En duelig Potetoptager.

1. "How can we get the potatoes up, Per, when we can't use Kate?" "Oh, we'll have to use the tractor."

2. "Aren't you going to use the plow?" "You're the same poor simpleton you've always been, Ola."

3. "Look here now — stand just like this and pay out the rope at the right speed."

Per som Læremester.

1. "You're like the 'contrary woman' in the fairytale, Ola. I always take the bark off before I chop down the oak." "Is that so?"

2. "This works just as fast as a dog eats fleas." "Did you ever see the like!"

3. "And that isn't all. It's so easy and up to date." "Oh yeah —"

4. "And how easy it is to get down again, ha ha!"

træktern — traktoren
look hare — sjå her

isi — lett
up-tu-dæ't — moderne

Naar Ford'n ſkal fixes.

1. "Can you help me fix the Ford today, Per?" "Yeah sure."

2. "What do you need to do with it?" "I have to fix something under the engine."

3. "I don't understand this patent." "You see, I'll cut the rope so the oak springs up and lifts it by the front."

"Hei, Ole! Nu er han færdig".

1. "Will you let me know, Lars, when Per is through oiling the windmill?" "Of course."

2. "Have you started oiling, Per?" "I'm almost through now, Lars."

3. "Dear me, Per, please be careful." "What do you take me for?"

4. "Hey, Ola! Now he's through."

---

fixe — reparere
injeina — motoren
katter — skjærer
lifter — løfter

vindmilla — vindmølla
vat yu tæk me for? — hva slags kar
   tror du jeg er?

1. "Oh, I have such a backache, Ola." "That's too bad, Per. But let me do as father used to do. He got someone to walk on his back with his knees, and then he got well again."

2. "Does it hurt, Per?" "Oh yes —"

3. "Just keep it up anyway."

4. "That's enough, now, Ola. Quit now — Can't you hear me? Stop, I say, you blasted nitwit."

1. "Oh, would you please get hold of a bottle of painkiller for me, Per — I feel so terrible today." "That'll be a simple matter, Ola."

2. "Won't it run at all?"

3. "It's just a wire that has slipped." "Oh is that all."

---

tu bæd — synd
painkiller — smertestillende middel
fila — føler meg

itte ætaal — slett ikke
wire — ledning
slippa — glidd ut
oh is that all — å, er det det hele

p. m. — ettermiddag (om klokkeslett)
rundt — i nærheten

Per tar feil af Blinken.

1. "Are you going to finish off the cat anyway now?" "I have to carry out my plans at last."

2. "Hold on — Now I think I have it straight." "Let 'er go."

4. "Ow! Ow!"

Han Ola og han Per er reist til Dakota.

1. "If you feel as I do, Per, we'll leave for Dakota with our thrashing rig." "Yes, I've been thinking about it all summer."

2. "Well, goodbye — have a good time."

---

hol' an - hold fast
let 'er go — la det smelle

treskeriggen — skurtreskeren
goodbye — farvel

1. " 'Travel east and west, But home is always best', tra la la —"

2. "I wanted to hear how Per is feeling after the long trip." "I can't understand where he is. I haven't seen him since we got back yesterday."

3. "Maybe he's gone to town." "Well, that beats everything! Look, there he is in the straw stack."

4. "Aren't you glad to be back home, Per?" "You coulda left me behind in Fargo, by thunder!!"

1. "Maybe we ought to test the boiler before we drive it into the shed, Ola." "We can just as well do it now as later."

2. "Shall we test it with the sledge hammer or with the crowbar, Per?" "You're just like your old self, Ola. Don't you understand that we have to use the steam test?"

3. "The pressure is two hundred pounds now, Per. You don't need to run it up any more." "If you're scared, Ola, you can go back home. I want to run it up to —"

---

trippen — turen
bitar — overgår (uttrykket "bitar grisen" er norsk-amerikansk for "går over all forstand")

straastakken — halmstakken
liva — etterlatt
bai tønder — (se ovenfor nr. 7)

bøiler'n — dampkjelen
shed'n — skuret
crobari — brekkjernet
steamtesten — dampprøven

pund — omtrent et halvt kilo
rønnen op — drive det (damptrykket) opp

1. "I thought that today we ought to divide up the thrashing money, Per. We can do it safely now that it's raining so hard. I have it here in my sack." "Yeah sure! Today we're safe, Ola."

2. "I'm starting to get hungry, Ola. Let's go out in the shanty and get a cup of coffee and a bite to eat." "That's the stuff, Per."

1. "I can't understand what Per is thinking about that he hasn't started plowing."

2. "Goodbye for a while, Ola. I'm going back up to Fargo to get something. Hee, hee, hee —"

3. Oh well, I suppose he went up to recover his wits."

After five or six days

4. "Hi, Ola! Here we are my boy! I and my wife!

---

sjur — javisst
sæf — trygg
shanti — kokeskuret

that's the stoff — det var en tipp-
     topp idé

1. "Won't you have some more chicken, Per?" "Oh yes indeed, my little dove."

2. "They talk about paradise on earth. That must be here, I should think —"

3. "Hol' on!"

1. "I'm afraid we won't get this Ford down again." "Oh sure."

2. "Look here now, Lars — When it falls down on the pole here, you adjust it so that the car slides down easy and doesn't go to pieces." "Of course I understand what you mean."

3. "Go ahead, Ola!"

chicken — kylling
hol' an — hold fast
look hare — sjå her
polen — stangen

sleide — gli
isi — langsomt
gaa hed — kjør i vei

Per og den "Traadløse".

1. "Oh, so you've bought yourself a wireless too now, Per." "Well, you see it was Polla who wanted it. She says they all have a wireless in Fargo. Would you have time to help me hook it up, Ola?"

2. "Is it strong, the board you're standing on, Per?" "Oh sure, I've nailed it on myself."

3. "Well, I'll be —"

4. "Can you hear a lot of interesting things, Per?"

"Der ſkal ſterk Lud til ſkurvede Hoder."

1. "What in the world are you doing, Per?" "Oh, I just wanted to wash my head in gasoline to get rid of this Dakota breed."

2. "My goodness, Per! That silken hair of yours might give off a spark and catch fire." "Oh shucks, Polla! I'm not a spark plug after all."

3. "Fire! Fire!"

---

weierless — trådløs (tidlig ord for "radio")
hook'n op — kople den sammen

gasoline — bensin
Dakota breed'n — Dakotayngelen (dvs lus)
spark — gnist

kætje fire — ta fyr
spark plug — tennplugg
feier — brann

Per tar Polla altfor bogstavelig.

1. "You must come in and dress up now, Per. You know we're going to the minister today for dinner." "Yes, but I don't know how to behave. I'm not used to such things."

2. "Now don't forget, Per, to do exactly as I do." "No, of course — but please, Polla, look out that you don't slip in the mud here."

3. "Ouch!"

4. "My heavens, are you crazy, man?" "Well, didn't you say I should do exactly as you did?"

En uheldig flytning.

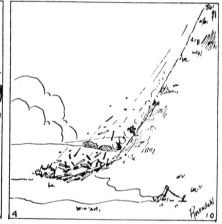

1. "How come you have to move your house, Per?" "Polla says there's too little view down below the hill. She thinks it's so pretty to watch the sun set."

2. "Giddap, Kate."

---

dresse op — kle deg om
behave mei — oppføre meg
auch — au

gedep — hypp hypp

1. "It'll be tough to live in the hen house this winter, Polla, but I guess there's nothing else we can do, since we got our house smashed up." "Just so I can be with you, Per, it will be allright."

2. "Gee whiz! It will be impossible to live there. It is chuck full of mites." "Terrible how those little pests bite! — I'll have to go to Ola and ask how we can get rid of them."

3. "All you have to do is to smear kerosine on the chicken roosts. Soak them real thoroughly." "Is that so?"

4. "Ah yes, now Per is busy killing chicken lice."

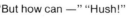

1. "Be quiet now, Ola, and I'll turn on the wireless."

2. "But how can —" "Hush!"

3. " — you manage —" "H · s · s · t"

4. " — to —" "Shut your trap —"

6. "Good-for-nothing humbug!!"

---

taaf — besværlig
leva — bo
smæsja op — knust, smadret
gee whiz — du verden

chuck fuldt — smekkfullt
mites — midd, lus
kerosine — parafin
soak dei in — gjennombløt dem

is dat so — jaså?
tørne paa — slå på

1. "Did you read the piece in the last *Decorah-Posten*, Per, about China? It says that a Chinese can have three wives —" "You don't say!"

2. "And a foreigner can have as many as he wants." "Oh my!"

Next morning

3. "It is so sad to say goodbye, but I have resolved to leave for China with the purpose of converting the people there and establishing peace."

4. "Who would have thought there was so big a heart in such a blockhead?" "Oh, Lars is not what he seems to be, I tell you, Ola. And he's not so dumb either. He's gone to school in Oslo and Berlin, and besides, he read seven years for the minister at confirmation."

1. "Here's a telegram from your brother."

2. "Per! Per! Bring some water!" "Oh, poor Lars — oh, poor Lars —" "Look and see what's wrong before you start raving."

3. "Ola, you read, I can't bear it."

4. "Hollywood, California. Dear Per! I decided to settle down as a missionary here instead of leaving for China. There are so many ungodly pretty girls here. Send me a thousand dollars or two.

Lars"

---

aa mai — å nei da

Her er det telegram fra bror din.
daler — (amerikansk) dollar

1. "Are you here, my dove? Today I guess you'll have to milk the cow yourself, now that Lars is away. I have to help Ola dig out a skunk."

2. "Oh, tra la la."

3. "Now if I only knew how I can get the milk to run out."

4. "Are you soon through, Polla?" "My goodness! I haven't even got her started up yet."

1. "This is a magnificent house you got built, but what kind of a patent is that on the wall there?" "That's one of those 'sleeping porches' that the big shots in Fargo use. We've just got the bed set up, so we're going to try it tonight."

2. "Maybe I should get out the wool quilt, Polla? It was thirtytwo below zero when I came in from the barn." "Just as you wish."

At dawn

3. "Per! Per! Your feet are frozen stiff."

4. "Well, I'll be darned if they aren't."

---

digge ut — grave ut
ein skunk — et stinkdyr
my goodness — jøsses

sleeping porch — soveveranda
ullkvilten — ullteppet
to aa tredive under nul — 36 kulde-
    grader (C°)

1. "You were late getting your wood driven in this year, Per." "Yes, I got so terribly behind with everything this winter."

2. "Hold on, boys! It could fall down on you. Let me tear some of it down."

3. "Look out everybody!" "I don't believe he can —"

4. "Ola! Ola!" "Well, did you ever see the like —"

1. "How come you're going to slaughter a pig now, Per?" "Well, it just happens that we're out of food. Polla's a big eater, I tell you, Ola."

2. "Well but how —" "Oh goodness! You don't understand anything, Ola. Go over to the end of this two-by-four and I'll show you."

3. "Have you got it into your head now?" "Yes, you bet! I can lift you with one hand, fellow."

4. "Ow, ow, Ola!"

beheind — forsinket
hol an — stopp
look out ever body — pass dere allesammen

aa gudnes — å bevares
tu-bai-forn — planke to tommer tykk og fire tommer bred (cirka 4 × 8 cm.)

ju bet — sjølsagt

1. "Is this some new kind of coffee grinder you've bought, Per?" "You're wrong again, Ola. This is a Belgian dish washer, of the very newest make, at that. They are so much in use in Fargo."

2. "Is that so? Is it from Belgium? Who would have thought that the blacks down south there would be so smart." "Is it ready to start up, Polla?" "Yes, dear, any time."

3. "Terrible how fast it moves!" "Just wait till I get it up to full speed, then you'll see —"

1. "Here it says in *Decorah-Posten,* Ola, that a Frenchman has discovered that if you want to bake potatoes and put a little nitroglycerine in each potato, you can loosen the skins." "Let's try that, Per."

2. "I wonder if a teaspoon in each potato is enough?" "I think that ought to do it, Per."

3. "They ought to be baked by the time we get back, Ola." "Yes sir, I fired up with dry oakwood."

4. "Gee whiz! Now the skins sure loosened in your potatoes, Ola."

---

belgien — belgisk
dish washer — diskemaskin
mæken — fabrikat, merke

yes dear any time — ja, kjære deg, når som helst
spid — fart

diskovra — oppdaga
feira op — fyrte opp

Per "brækker ind" Pollas Ridehest.

1. "How do you like the pony I bought for Polla? I'm gonna break him in now, he's so very nice." "He looks as patient as a lamb."

2. "You better pull back, Ola, in case he should buck a little at first."

3. "Whoa, whoa!"

4. "Whoa, whoa!"

5. "Whoa, whoa!"

6. "Whoa, you fool —"

En Feil i Indretningen.

1. "Hey, Ola! Come in and go upstairs with me, so you can see a handy arrangement."

2. "It's one of these chutes for dropping dirty clothes into. Go down in the cellar and see how nicely they slide down." "That's certainly clever."

3. "I can't see anything, Per." "Wait a minute, Ola. It's clogged up here —"

4. "Oh my, oh dear!"

---

poni'n — ponnien
riebrekke'n (break him in for riding) — ri han inn

ho — ptro
yu ful — din idiot

opstærs — ovenpå
hændig — hendig, praktisk
chute — styrtsjakt

sleider — glir
clogga op — tetta igjen

1. "How do you intend to move the silo, Per?" "I intend to lay it on its side and then run the tractor inside it and sort of roll it up the hill."

2. "You better take with you a post, Ola, to lay under it if the engine should stop when I get up the hill." "Yeah, sure."

3. "The engine stopped, Ola. Lay the post under it quick."

4. "Wait a little, Per, I have to find more to lay under it."

1. "Isn't it strange that we are so well agreed, Polla? I think definitely that we must be soul mates." "Well, we haven't anything to disagree about, either."

2. "Yes dear, but I didn't say we disagreed. I just said —" "You said it was strange that we were such good friends. Exactly as if —"

3. "My goodness, Polla, you misunderstand —" "I understand that you don't care for me — I understand — boo hoo — "

4. "Boo hoo."

---

træktern — traktoren
ein post — en stolpe
injein — motoren
ja sjur — ja vel

soul mates — sjelsfrender
my goodness — kjære deg
kæra — bryr deg

Per paa Reise til Afrika.

1. "Whoa, back!"

2. "Where are you going, Per?" "I'm going to Africa."

3. "Are you crazy, Per? What in the world is wrong?" "Polla has left me, gone to Fargo. I want to get away, away from everything —"

4. "Per! Per! Wait a while. I want to talk with you."

Per paa Hungerstreik.

1. "What's the matter with Per?" "He's gone on a hunger strike and swears that he won't eat until he gets his Polla back. We're bound to get some nourishment into him."

2. "We'll try to get some of this gruel here into 'im."

3. "Now you hold 'im, boys." "Blub, blub."

4. "You can go to the devil."

---

ho bæk — ptro
liva — forlatt

baund te — nødt til
hunger streik — sultestreik

Per er en uforbederlig "Flirt".

1. "Hey Ola! Here's a telegram from Polla. She's coming back home today. Now I'm going to the depot to meet 'er." "Is that so! Ha - ha -ha."

2. "But isn't this beautiful weather today, Per?" "Yeah, you bet, Polla." "Hello, Per."

3. "Hello?"

4. "I'll teach you, you old rascal!"

En slem "Mistake".

1. "Yankee doodle dandy —"

2. "Tra - la - la - la - la -"

4. "Oh, excuse me, Ola. I thought it was Per coming." "Haw haw haw! That was a good joke on you, Ola."

---

depon — stasjonen
is dat so — jaså ja
ju bet — javisst

"Yankee doodle ..." — amerikansk sang
excuse — unnskyld
jok — puss

Per er altid lige uheldig.

1. "What are you up to, Per?" "Oh, I was trying to get back on her feet a cow that can't stand up. It's a good thing you came to help me, Ola."

2. "Whoa! That's enough."

3. "Whoa! Whoa! Are you crazy, Ola!" "I can't stop it. Where's the brake at?"

Han Ola har det travlt.

1. "Oh, would you help tip over this old straw stack, Ola. I'm afraid it might fall on the cow." "I'm terribly busy today, Per, but I s'pose I better go with you."

2. "I'll take out the support, and then —" "Well, but you have to hurry up."

3. "Wait a minute, Ola." "Here she goes."

4. "Ola! Ola!" "Now I just have to go, Per."

brekken — bremsen
tippe — velte
bisi — opptatt

hørri op — skynde deg
hare she goes — her går den
baund — nødt

Pers nyeste Patent.

1. "Oh so this is the trolley you talked about. But isn't it dangerous to ride on it, Per?" "Oh no, Ola! You take hold of the crank, and I'll sit down and take a ride."

2. "Not so fast, Ola." " Uff!"

3. "Hold on, Ola! Hold on!"

4. "Gosh!"

Et gammelt "Trick", som mislykkedes.

1. "Wait a minute, Ola. I can handle fellows like that."

2. "Stand outside the gate here, and I'll frighten the wits out of this lousy dog. I know a trick that never fails." "Really?"

3. "B - r - r - r" "G - r - r - woof —"

4. "Haw haw haw —" " Ow, ow, Ola!"

---

trolley'n — løypestrengen
ride — kjøretur
hol' an — hold igjen
gosh — jøsses

hændle — klare
trik — knep

Det er "taaf" at være Per.

1. "It'll be tough to knock loose those boards, Per." "Oh my no, Ola. You just take this oak plank here and go inside and knock them out."

2. "It's going all right, man!" "Yes, I knew that already."

3. "I can't get this board here loose." "Oh, just push with all your might."

4. "Hooray! Now it came loose!"

Polla er jalour paa Per.

1. "I hear they voted you in as clerk of our school district. Congratulations!" "Well, you see there was nobody else in the district who could handle that job."

2. "But what do you actually have to do? Is it writing and things like that?" "Oh sure! I have to answer the letters from all the schoolmams who apply for jobs, write to the superintendent, to the county nurse, to the farm bureau, to the weed inspector etc. etc."

3. "Who are you writing to, Per?" "Oh, I have to answer the letter I got from Miss Olson. She's applying —"

4. "Miss Olson! Miss Olson! Nothing doing, Per!"

taaf — vanskelig	vota — stemte	æppleier — søker	farm bjuro'n — landbrukskontoret
inside — innafor	clerk — sekretær	superintenten — skoleinspektøren	weed — ugras
aalreit — fint, bra	hændle — klare	kaunti nursen — fylkessykesøstra	miss — frøken
	skolemammene — lærerinnene		

1. "What kind of a patent have you made now again, Per?" "It's a kind of 'knock out' grubbing machine that I read about in *Decorah-Posten*."

2. "I don't understand at all — " "Well, I'll explain, Ola. All you have to do is to drive straight at the stump with full speed and knock it to pieces. We'll drive over to the grub and try it."

3. "Look out, Ola!"

4. "Oh, was that the little stump you were aiming at?"

Per paa gale Veie.

1. "Hello, Ola!" "Oh hello, Polla. So you're at home. I thought you were with Per when I met him a while ago."

2. "Did Per have a woman with him?" "I don't know if it was a woman or a girl. But it was a female."

3. "They were going north on the Jefferson Highway."

---

knock out — slå ut
grubbe machine — stubbebryter
explæne — forklare
spid — fart

grubben —nybrøytet
look out — pass deg
heivei — riksveg

1. "Here's a telegram from *Decorah-Posten*, Per. They've run short of pictures. We could have waited with the reaping and tended to this business, as I said." "Well, we'll have to hurry home and see if we have any, then."

2. "We'll take the shortcut across the Smith land, Ola." "Yes, I think so, too."

4. "What does it say on that sign, Ola?" "It says we should stay away from this place."

1. "We're bound to have two men to measure the grain. One man can't manage it by himself." "That's right." "Haw! Haw! Haw! Now I've never heard the like. Let me take that job, Ola."

2. "Hey Ola! I've seen worse things than this, I can tell you."

3. "Maybe we're not pitching fast enough for you, Per?" "Keep 'er going."

4. "You'd better slow down a little, boys. I'm almost out of empty sacks."

liva — venta med
ripinga — innhøstinga
tenda te — tatt oss av
detta bisnesse — denne saka
Smith land'e — Smiths jord

signe — skiltet
Notice: horses and mules keep off
   — ingen adgang for hester og muldyr

that's right — det er sant
pitja — kaste (med høygaffel)
keep 'er going — driv bare på
slo'e paa — saktne på farten
ute ta — sloppet opp for

Per "græduater" i Biehold.

1. "Hello, Polla! Is Per at home today?" "Oh sure, he's busy with his lessons."

2. "What kind of lessons? Has he started reading for the minister again?" "No, not at all. He's taking one of these correspondence courses in beekeeping."

3. "I wonder where that rascal is. Hey, Per!"

4. "How's it going, Per. Will you graduate soon?" "I'm busy on the last lesson, Ola."

Polla fik nok af "Rubbedoktoren".

1. "Are you taking a trip, Per?" "Oh, I'm just taking Polla down to Davenport to a 'rubbing doctor'. Her back hurts her so."

2. "Per! Per! Ouch ouch!"

3. "By golly, this is going too far!" "Ouch, ouch!"

4. "Now you can rub —"

---

ja sjur — javisst
correspondence course — brevkurs
beekeeping — biehold

græduate — ta eksamen
Davenport — by i staten Iowa
rubbedoktor — (folkelig uttrykk for)
   massør, kiropraktiker

rubbe — gni
by golly — søren

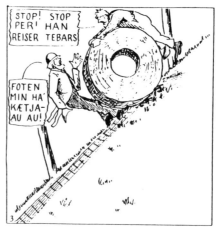

1. "Shall we roll off this fence up the hill, then?" "That was the idea, Ola!"

2. "Well, now the worst is over, Ola." "We're almost there now."

3. "Stop, stop, Per! It's going backwards." "My foot has caught. Ouch, ouch!"

4. "Hold on! Hold on! Are you crazy, Ola?"

1. "What best sustains us when life is dreary,
And when our way seems long and weary —
Is that our future is concealed,
And what will happen unrevealed."

2. "Yes alas, our future is unknown, but anyhow I know that I will get a warm reception at Per's house."

3. "My goodness! A tramp again."

4. "Ouch! Ouch!"

---

detta fence — dette gjerdet
kætja — hengt seg fast
hol' an — stopp

anyhow — allikevel
my goodness — gubbevars
en tramp — en fant

1. "Oh, Lars. Today you can tear down that straw shed over there. I and Ola are going around to collect grass widow pensions." "But be careful, Lars, so you leave the corner posts to the end." "Oh, don't worry, Ole. I've taken down lots of sheds like this in my day."

2. "I wonder if this stupid Ole really thinks that he can teach me anything."

3. "This is no trick at all."

4. "Help, help!"

1. "What shall I do today, Per?" "I thought you could try pruning the appletrees today, Lars."

2. "Look here now — you cut off the branches that —" "Of course, of course. That's just what should be done."

4. "So I'm finally through with that miserable job."

---

straashed'e — halmløa
kollekte — samle inn
græswiddo — grasenke
ta kær — pass på

liver — lar vente med
corner — hjørne
don't vørri — aldri bry deg
prune — beskjære

ikke no' triks ætall — slett ikke
   noen kunst
prune — beskjære

look hare — sjå her
katter — skjærer

1. "I wonder what this means?" "That's nothing to wonder about, Per. 'Danger bridge' means that there is something dangerous about the bridge, and 'out' means that everybody has to keep out of this territory."

2. "You better back up, Ola, and turn around —"

3. "Good land! We haven't got the time to turn back. We have to keeping driving straight ahead."

1. "Now I really don't know what I'm gonna do, Ola. The butcher phoned down that I should bring up that cow today, but goodness, how can we —" "You can't even think of it, Per. We're bound to tend to this other business."

2. "Can't I do it, Per? You know I was a bit of a cowboy in my younger days." "That's just fine, Lars. Polla can go with you and drive 'er."

3. "Come boss, come boss."

4. "Whoa boss!! Whoa! Whoa!"

---

danger bridge out — fare, brua er borte
territory — strøk
bæke op — rygge

good land — du slette tid
straight ahead — rett fram

butcher'n — slakteren
fona — ringte
gudness — herregud
baund te — nødd til

tende — passe, ta oss av
bisnese — saken
bas — kyra

1. "If you have the time, Lars, you can drain off the old oil from the tractor and fill it up with fresh." "Yes, I'll be glad to, Per."

2. "It's that screw under here you have to take out if you —" "I'm not born today, Ole."

3. "Now at last I got it loose."

4. "How are things going, Lars, are you managing?" "Blub, blub."

1. "Oh say, Polla, would you please cut Lars's hair today and trim his beard. He looks so tough." "Oh sure."

2. "But wouldn't it be a good idea to cut the beard all the way off. It's just too long. "Yes indeed, that's just what I was thinking, too."

3. "Please, Polla, don't make it too short."

4. "Ow! Ow! Ow! You took the tip of my nose —" "What do I care?"

---

træktern — traktoren
say — hør
taaf — barsk
idea — idé

katte — skjære
what do I care — hva bryr jeg meg
   om det

Lars er ude for et svinagtigt Uheld

1. "Would you mind doing a good deed for Lars, Polla, and mend his pants? He can't go around like this all Christmas." "Sure, just lay it in the doorway here until I'm ready." "You can lay it here until we come back, and then we'll take it back to Lars."

3. "Wasn't that just like Per? He forgot to leave Lars's pants."

4. "Per! Ole! Come back with my trousers! It's so awfully cold."

Hvorledes Lars turede Julen.

1. "Say, Ola, you wouldn't have an overall to lend Lars so he can go to town and send in the grasswidow pension we've collected? We've got thirty dollars and ninety nine cents." "Yes, that's fine, Per. We don't have time to fool any more with it anyway.".

2. "If you wish, Lars, you can borrow money from the pension fund to buy yourself a pair of pants." "I thank you."

3. "Hello, Lars! Now you're just in time. I have some extra good stuff here that I got from Canada." "Well, it has certainly been a dry, sad Christmas this year. Fix up an order for thirty dollars and ninety-nine cents."

4. "It is morning on the hillside, There is sunshine on the knoll, It is starlight on the ocean, But there's moonshine on my soul. Tra la la la la."

---

leave — legge igjen
say — hør
overhal — overalls
fule — tulle

just in time — i rette tid
(verset:) 'Det er morgensol i lia, det er solskinn oppå haugen, det er stjerner over havet, men i min

sjel er det måneskinn (= heimebrent).

Per3 "Patentkrank."

1. "I can't get the truck started today, Per. You'll have to come and help me." "I'll take and put this patent crank on it, so you can be sure to start it."

2. "But how can you make it —" "Just wait a little, Ola, and then you'll see."

3. "Keep it in neutral now, Lars, and then we'll crank it both behind and in front." "Of course I already have my foot in neutral, my good Per."

En Kalv paa Afveie.

1. "This good-for-nothing calf has got its head in the wheel and I can't get it out again." "Find a piece of a log and put it under the axle, and then drive the tractor over. Quick now, Ola."

2. "All right, sir. Start 'er up." "Yes, but how in the wide world — ??"

3. "Step up the speed, Ola. Now it'll fly out soon."

trøkken — lastebilen
krænken — sveiven
nutræl — frigir

krænke'n — sveive, starte med håndsveiv

kvik — fort, kvikt
allreit sir, start 'er up — all right, start 'n opp
spid — fart

1. "Have you any idea, Per, how many checker games we have played?" "Oh goodness, I haven't kept track. But isn't it strange that we have always remained friends."

2. "It's nice of you to let me take three in one move. Ha, ha, now I even get a king." "Hol' on! Hol' on! That wasn't fair —"

3. "Maybe you think I cheated, too?" "I have to believe what I see with my own eyes after all, you con —"

4. "— founded scoundrel."

1. "It's terrible that it's raining like this right in the middle of winter." "Yeah, I'll be soaked as a herring by the time I get home."

2. "Go get me a pail of water, Per. You're wet anyway, now."

3. "Look out!"

4. "Now you're wet, too, Polla. Now you can go and get the water yourself."

---

checker gamer — damspill
keepa træk — holdt rede
ein shoot — ett trekk
hol' an — stopp

fair — rettferdig
cheata — snytt
en pail — ei bøtte
look out — pass deg

Da Lars blev "fumigæta"

1. "What should I help you with today, Per?" "Oh, we have to disinfect Lars and let him out again. The doctor said that he has gotten over the smallpox enough so he doesn't have to be quarantined any longer."

2. "But is Lars supposed to be inside the house when you smoke it?" "Oh sure, you see it's full of those worms on him. They're in his hair, his face, his clothes, his shoes, and all over."

3. "I s'pose it's these microbes you mean. What kind of disinfectant are you using?" "Oh, I'm using sulphur."

4. "I think this ought to do it now, Per." "Oh good gracious, Ola! We have to keep it up for twelve hours at least."

Jamen var "Jupiter" olm lel.

1. "This bull of yours won't be easy to get home again, Per. He's — no no, don't cross the fence, Per." "Oh, this rascal is not so bad. He's so gentle I can lead him with my little finger."

2. "Come Jupiter, come Jupiter —"

4. "Haw! haw! haw! What did I tell him!"

---

disinfekte — desinfisere
small pox'n — småkoppene
quaranteina — i karantene
sjur — sjølsagt

worms — makk
al over — overalt
microbes — bakterier
disinfektent — desinfeksjonsmiddel

good græshus — herregud
fumigæta — desinfisert ved røyking

keepe de' op — holde på
æt least — i det minste
bul'n — oksen
fence — gjerdet

117

Lars ved nok hvad han snakker om

1. "If you're through with the chores, Lars, you can go out on the pond and saw loose some ice. I and Ola are going to drive it home this afternoon." "When I'm through feeding the pigs their hay, I'll be ready."

2. "Be careful, Lars, and stay on solid ice while you're sawing." "Oh, I'm old enough to know where I have to stand, Ole, and in any case, I helped them saw ice out there in Hollywood."

Hvorledes Per og Ola fanger Bjørn

1. "Here it says that you catch bears if you soak a rag in alcohol and hang it over the trap. It'll go for miles for that smell, it says." "It doesn't cost much to try it. I saw the tracks of a bear up in the north grub yesterday."

2. "It would be a good joke if we caught it at last." "If I don't misread the signs, we'll have bear steak for dinner tomorrow."

At dawn

3. "By jiminy! We've caught it, man!"

---

chors'a — fjøsstellet	*kætje* — fange	*joke* — puss
feeda — fora	*soker* — bløter	*grubben* — oppbrutt land
kærful — forsiktig	*træppa* — fella	*bai jimini* — jøsses au
	træksa — spora	*kætja* — fanga

Skunken blev vond paa Per

1. "Are you trying to hide, Per?" "Oh, I was just wondering how I could get hold of some eggs under here."

2. "Can't you just crawl under? I can pull you out again by your feet." "You're not helpless, are you, Ola."

3. "Ouch! Ouch! Ola, pull me out —ouch —quick — ouch — gosh!!"

4. "Haw! haw! haw! Oh, gee whiz."

Per tog ikke Lars i Betragtning

1. "Good land! What's the matter, Per?" "Oh, I just took out my liberty bonds from the bank. There are so many bank robberies that I didn't dare leave them there any longer."

2. "Do you have a safer place than the bank to put them in?" "Yes, you bet I have."

3. "I know that nobody can find them here."

4. 12:30 A.M. "Help, help!"

---

gee whiz — gubbevars	*good land* — gode gud	*sæfere* — tryggere
skunken — stinkdyret	*liberty bonds* — statsobligasjoner	*ju bet* — ja visst
kvik — fort	*bænkrobberis* — bankrøverier	
ouch — au	*live* — la være, la stå	

Lars atter paa Rangelen

1. "Have you turned over to the sheriff that jug of moonshine that we took the other day, Per?" "I've just got Lars to take it with him to town."

4. "Oh, I hear your voice, but I can't help you."

Lars blir bukselaus igjen

1. "Where's that rascal Lars at? I'm bound to get back those pants I lent him." "He went over in the Sour Apple Valley and isn't back yet."

2. "Oh, I see!"

3. "Well, well, be that as it may. The pants are mine."

---

tørna over — gitt over
sheriffen — lensmannen
jaaggen — dunken

moonshein — heimebrent
baund te — nødt til
oh I see — nå ser jeg

1. "I think it's so sad that we have to go around the community and beg for money to buy Lars a new pair of pants, but how —?" "Oh, sure it's sad, I suppose, but he can't go around like this in the spring thaws."

2. "How do you do, Mrs. Jones. My, but you got some dandy place here —. I wish I was as well off." "We won't waste your time, Mrs. Jones, but you see, I and Ola are around collecting some money for Lars, my brother —"

3. "Here Rover, here Rover."

4. "Sic em, Rover."

1. "Is Lars going on a trip?" "Yes, he's going to New York to go to a school of chiropractic."

2. "These chiropractors are going to run the other doctors entirely out of business." "Gulp, gulp."

3. "It seems there's something to this chiropractic cure after all."

4. "Yes indeed. Polla got well after she took just one adjustment."

My, but you got some dandy place here — Du verden, så fin en gard du har her
sic em — puss ta'm

keiropræktik — kiropraktikk
keiroprækteran — kiropraktikkerne
adjustment — behandling

En slem Feiltagelse

1. "But how are we gonna get 'im out again, Ola?" "Oh, we'll smoke him out. You stay here and watch him, Per, while I go and get some dry straw."

2. "It shouldn't be any trick to pull him out again by the tail."

3. "Per must have gone back home, but I'll light up anyway and see how things go."

4. "Ola! Ola! Are you crazy, man!"

Et udmerket Middel mod Agenter

1. "What kind of a machine do you have here, Per?" "Oh, it's one of these 'Protectors', so to speak, against salesmen. There are getting to be so many of them — By jimini, there comes one now."

2. "How do you do, sir — My name is Softsnap — I represent The Bunkum Life Insurance Company — I am —" "Yas, yas."

3. "Excuse me a minute. I'll be back here right away. Just stand where you are." "All right, sir."

4. "Call again, please."

---

itte no trik — ingen kunst
protector — beskytter
saa tu spik — så å si
bai jimini — herregud

Agenten: God dag, mitt navn er Softsnap. Jeg representerer livsassuranseselskapet Bunkum. Jeg er —

Per: Unnskyld et øyeblikk. Jeg kommer straks tilbake. Bare stå der du står. Kom igjen, er du snill.

Per Kloroformerer fig felv

1. "Oh say, Ola, do you know how they use chloroform? I was going to put an end to old Watch today." "You take and put Watch into a tight box, and then you lay a rag by his nose and pour on chloroform."

2. "Hello, Polla. How did it go? Did Per get Watch killed today?" "He's been at it all day, so I think he ought to be through with it now. I think he's over by the barn somewhere."

4. "Well, that beats everything! If that idiot isn't sitting in the box himself?"

Ola anede noget galt var paafærde

1. "We can't make this oak fall to the north, Per." "That's the worst of it. Knock in a wedge on the south side, Ola."

2. "This will never in the world work." "Oh sure, it will work."

3. "Yes, but it could jump off the stump." "Go ahead, go ahead!"

---

aa say — hør
ein baxt — ei kasse
killa — drept
barn — fjøset

bitar — overgår
wedge — blei
gaa hed — driv på

Per kommer forsent til Toget.

1. "I'll go down to the depot, Per, when I'm ready. Then you can follow with my suitcase." "Yes, sure, I'll be there on time, Polla."

2. "Are you going away, Per?" "No, it's Polla who's going up to Fargo to her mama and stay there this summer. She hasn't been feeling well this spring, you see, so she wanted a change of climate."

3. "By thunder! Now I hear the train —." "Now you'll have to rush, my boy."

4. "Whoa! Whoa! Stop!!"

"Saa fær døkk ha gubbei da," sier'n Per og han Ola.

1. "What have you been planning to do today, Per." "I'm planning to take a vacation. I'm going up to a relative I have in Canada and do nothing but hunt and fish. You better join me, Ola. It beats everything how much wind this tire takes."

2. "But is it necessary to take a bed with us?" "Well, you see, we have to camp out, and I can't stand to lie on the bare ground."

3. "You're not planning to take with you a cow, are you?" "Oh you surely see that we have to have milk on the way, and anyway it's uncertain if they have cows in Canada."

4. "They must not have dragged the road here this spring." "No, it looks as if they forgot that."

---

depon — stasjonen
suitkesen min — kofferten min
on teim — i tide
fila — følt seg

chænge av klimat — klimaforandring
treine — toget
ho — ptro

plæna — planlagt
vækæsjen — ferie
hunte — gå på jakt
de' bitar alt — det går over all forstand

teiern — ringen
kæmpe — kampe, slå leir
drægge raaden — jevnet vegen
gubbei — farvel

1. "Ola! Ola!"

2. "I can't stand walking any farther — This dreadful stomach ailment — I want Polla to have the farm — and then I want to give ten dollars to grass widows' pension — and five to —" "Oh shut up, you idiot!"

3. "Now I'm telling you, Per, I don't want to hear any more nonsense."

4. "Now we have just a mile left to the border and then we're saved."

1. "Now you can cheer up, Per, now we can see home."

2. "Hurry up now." "Yes, yes, Ola — But we're quite played out, both I and the cow."

3. "Now they've foreclosed the mortgage and sold your farm, Per. Ha, ha, ha! That's a good joke on you. Now you're homeless for the winter, too. Ha, ha, ha!"

4. "If you had nothing more to faint for, you could have let it be."

---

farmen — garden	*ei mil* — (amerikansk) mil, dvs 7 km	*cheere up* — opp med humøret	*joke* — puss
daler — dollar	*lina* — grensa	*utplaya* — utkjørt	Notisen: Advarsel til Per: Hold deg
græswiddo — grasenke		*foreclosa mortgagen* — oppsagt	borte, farmen er solgt
shut up — hold kjeft		pantelånet	

1. "Well, I'll be darned if my wife Mari hasn't returned from Norway!"

2. "Now I'd really like to get a kiss from her, too. It's strange about old love, it never rusts."

4. "I think there must be a little rust on their love after all. Ha, ha, ha, ha!" "Mari! Mari! Are you crazy?" "Shut your mouth — You good-for-nothing loafer — I'll give you — It looks like a pigsty!" "Ow, ow!"

1. "Well, sirree, Ola. Now I've rented the McOlson farm, and I'll start in right away putting the house in shape so I can move in." "Is that so. Yes, Per, you're a hustler. If you wish, Mari and I can go with you and help."

2. "I made them give me a good bargain on the farm, too, I'll tell you, Ola." "Yes, I'll believe that, or what do you think, Mari?" "Oh, sure."

3. "Oh, good gracious! Help, Ola! Help! Help!"

loafer — lathans	*i sjæp* — i stand	*mæka* — tvang
skunk — stinkdyr	*move* — flytte	*good græshus* — herregud
renta — leid	*is dæt so* — jaså	
reit ævei — med en gang	*høsler* — driftig kar	

1. "What are you doing today, Per?" "Oh, I'm bound to catch Jupiter. It is not legal now to let the bulls go loose. Go back, Ola, and don't show yourself, and then I'll fool him into coming here."

2. "Bø — ø - ø, bu — u — u"

3. "Hurrah! Hurrah!" "Whee! Now you have him."

1. "What do you think of the mule I bought, Ola?" "He doesn't look too bad, but mules are so likely to kick."

2. "Oh no, this is one of those non-kicking mules." "Oh, really?"

3. "See here, it says in black on white, 'Warranted not to kick.'" "My goodness."

bullan — oksene
baund te — nødt til
kætje — fange
mjul'n — muldyret

non-kicking — som ikke sparker
warranted not to kick — garantert
   at den ikke sparker
my goodness — du verden

1. "Hi, Ola! Today Polla is coming home. She has her mama with her, too." "You don't say!"

2. "I suppose you'll be going to the depot to meet them." "Yes, sure. They're coming on the three-thirty train. I'm longing to meet my mother-in-law. I haven't seen her before."

3. "Oh, he'll get well acquainted with his mother-in-law, all right, ha ha."

4. 4 PM. "Ugh, what an ugly country you have here, Polla." "Oh, I think it's pretty."

1. "I thought I'd come over here and see if you needed any help, but I see you're already in running order." "Yes, I'll tell you, Ola, that Værmor is one who doesn't sit and twiddle her thumbs. She's — " "Hey Per! Hurry up!"

2. "I have to have some water to prime this good-for-nothing pump. It won't draw." "You can go and prime yourself, Per."

3. "Hold on, Værmor — "

4. "— Hold on! Hold on!"

depon — jernbanestasjonen
sjur — sjølsagt
treine — toget
kontri — landskap

rønning order — full stand
hurry up — skynd deg
hol' an — stopp, ta det med ro
prime — fylle på, spe på

1. "It's too bad to chop down this fine cottonwood oak, Per." "Yes, but I don't dare leave it. You see, it could blow down on the house."

2. "It's just about not necessary to fasten a rope on it, Ola." "Oh yes, it's safer."

3. "It was when I was in the pineries that I learned to cut the trees so that they fell exactly where I wanted to have them." "Oh, sure."

Per got the wrong "chicken"

1. "Oh, Per, will you take your gun and shoot this old rooster, so I can fix it up for dinner. Mamma can help you." "Yas, yas, my dear."

3. "All right." "Sh — h. Stand still. Now I've got 'im in my sights."

4. "Ow! Ow! Are you crazy, man! Can't you see the difference between my legs and an old rooster?"

---

cottonwoodeik — en slags amerikansk poppel
liv'a — la den stå

sæfere — tryggere
peinri — furuhogst

fixe'n — lage den til
yas — ja

Hvorledes Per "trainer Mjulen".

1. "Hey, Per, what's the matter?" "I'm gonna knock the stuffings out of this confounded mule."

2. "I think he'll be pretty tame when the performance is over." "Oh sure."

3. "T — r — r — r"

4. "Ha — ha — ha."

Per paa Nippet at bli' overkjørt

1. "It's awful how much work they put into this new highway." "Oh, it's just nonsense the whole thing."

2. "Hey, man! Here I found a pack of cigarettes." "Get out of the road, Per. Here comes a car."

3. "Per! Per!"

4. "It was that nasty bumper that hit you, Per." "That was just what saved me, Ola. If it hadn't been for the bumper, I would have got a real blow."

---

knocke stoffinga tor — gi grundig bank, banke opp
performance — forestilling
treine — trene
mjul'n — muldyret
heivein — riksvegen
ein car — ein bil
bumpern — støtfangeren
sæva — redda

1. "Are you trying to train your mule again, Per?" "You bet I'll train him. There'll be a real upset, I think, when I've lighted this rag that I've soaked in gasoline. Now you can kick, you rascal."

2. "This could go wrong, Per." "Haw, haw! Haw, haw!"

3. "Whoa back! Whoa back!"

1. "Now you have to go with me to the depot, Ola, and meet the chiropractor, my brother Dr. Lars. He's graduated from the school in New York, and he's quite soaked through, so to speak, with the science of chiropractic. The band will play, and the mayor will give the speech of welcome." "Really?"

2. "There really are a lot of people at the depot." "That's not strange, Ola, when so famous a man as Lars comes home."

3. "Yankee doodle dandy." The conductor: "Sh-h-psh S-sh-s"

4. "Well, what do you say now? It looks like he's soaked all right."

treina — trener
soke — bløyter
gasolin — bensin
whoa back — ptro

depon — jernbanestasjonen
græduata — tatt eksamen
soka — gjennombløtt, (her også) full

bænden — bandet, hornorkesteret
majorn — ordføreren

1. "But isn't it a lot of work to treat the posts with creosote, Per?" "Well, you see, I have to dip each post in this hot creosote, and of course, it does take some time."

2. "Aha! Moonshine, by jingo! That Ola is a real rascal who gets Per mixed up in that kind of wretched stuff. But just wait, I'll fix you."

3. "Phew! What awful stuff!"

1. "Here comes Per." "Hurrah for Per." "Clear the way, everybody." "Shucks."

2. "Hurrah!"

3. "Hey!!" "Oh yeah, I think I'll go home."

4. "You better get up now. I'm not going any farther."

---

trite — behandle
post — stolpe
creosote — kreosot (olje)

moonshine — heimebrent
by jingo — fanken au
I'll fix you — jeg skal ta meg av deg

clear the way, everybody — av veien, allesammen
shucks — tull

En radikal Gigtkur

1. "Where's Per at?" "He's over by the barn taking a cold bath for his rheumatism, I think."

2. "I'll go and ask him to come." "Oh well, I can wait here."

3. "Ola! Ola! Come quick! Per has frozen solid in the tank."

4. "My, how are we gonna get him loose?" "Oh my! Oh my!" "Oh, we'll get him loose all right when I get the ice chopped up."

Svigermor er i slet Lune

1. "Please, Polla, would you cook some cream porridge for dinner? I feel so poorly today." "Mamma can do that. I want to go to church today, Per."

2. "Come and stir the porridge, Per. I have to have more flour." "Sure, sure."

3. "Well, if I don't think that scoundrel is letting the porridge burn!"

4. "There you are — help yourself." "Oh, gee whiz."

---

barn — fjøset
oh my — å nei
fila — føler meg

there you are — help yourself —
  værsågod, forsyn deg
gee whiz — herregud

En virkningsfuld Medicin

1. "Look here, Ola, I've bought a bottle of what they call 'gland medicine'. It's guaranteed to cure all kinds of illnesses and will make a man as good as new." "Oh, but can this be possible?"

2. Next day — "Do you know, Polla, where that medicine I bought yesterday is at?" "Oh, mama took it and poured it into the pig trough."

3. "That beats everything! Værmor has given the pigs my medicine. Now I s'pose they're all dead, by thunder!" "Yes, but you can make her responsible, Per."

Svigermor greier det alene

1. "Hello, Ola. Come with your gun, quick. There's a tramp in my barn. Call up the neighbors, my goodness—" "Hide yourself, mama." "Phooey!"

2. "It's a terrible big one. He aimed right at my head —" "Did he have a pistol, then?"

3. "Good gracious, Værmor — Go back home!!" "Phooey."

4. "Help! Help!"

---

gland — kjertel
kure — kurere
bitar — overgår
bai tønder — jøsses

hello — hallo
tramp — fant
kal' op — ring
my gudnes — søren au

good græshus — herregud
help — hjelp

En seiglivet Okse

1. "Mari said you had phoned over there today. Was there anything you wanted, Per?" "Yes, I'm going to butcher Jupiter. And he's going to get a hard blow. I've laid dynamite under his feed box here, so I'll blow his whole head off."

2. "Now you can light the fuse, Per. Jupiter's by the feed box."

3. "Well well, so now your struggles are over. Goodbye, Jupiter, now you're no longer here." "I suppose we'd better start skinning him right away."

Atter en vaad Modtagelse

1. "Will it be all right, Polla, if I invite Lars, the doctor, for supper. I'd like to make him acquainted with Værmor."

2. "Poor Per, he has a pretty miserable home."

3. "Where shall I throw out the slop water, Polla?" "Oh, throw it out through the door."

---

fona — ringt
feedbaxten — krybba

inviter — ber, inviterer
supper — aftensmat

"Mjulen" kommer tilkort

1. "I'll be away all day today, Polla. That angry mule is loose in the cow pen, so you mustn't go there."

4. "I'll teach you, you old beast!"

En daarlig "Joke"

1. "Haw haw haw — My that was a good joke, Ola. I must tell that one to Værmor — haw haw haw."

2. "Do you know, Værmor, that Adam had the first talking machine, Eve — "

3. "Then came Edison and invented one you can stop. Haw haw haw haw — "

---

mjuln — muldyret
kupen — innhegningen for kuer

inventa — oppfant

Ogsaa et Forlig

1. "I've now decided, Ola, that I'm going to call together these women in our congregation that are always quarreling and see if I can't arrange for a reconciliation." "Yes, it's too bad they keep on in this way."

2. "I'll start by getting Mrs. Jones and Mrs. McOlson together first." "Yeah, they're sort of the leaders."

4. "How did it go, Per? Did you get Mrs. Jones and Mrs. McOlson together?" "Oh yes, now they're together."

Lars kommer i Unaade hos Svigermor

1. "It's quite unbelievable that you can be Polla's mama. You look just as young as the daughter. He he." "Do you think so, Dr. Lars, hee hee."

3. "If you think you can treat me in such a shameless way, you're badly mistaken, — you —"

4. "— dirty pig!"

Mrs. (missis) — fru
trite — behandle
dirty pig — skittengris

1. "We certainly have the wolf here, but we can't get 'im out." "I'll try crawling in here, Ola, and I'll scare 'im out, so you can kill 'im when he comes."

2. "One — two —"

3. "three — four —"

4. "five —" "Ow, ow!"

1. "It's wonderful how good you are at making things, Per." "Oh, I'm not too bad at puttering around, you see."

2. "What are you making there?" "Oh, it's — you see — I just was thinking—"

3. "Oh say, Værmor—"

4. "Good gracious, what a fool."

say du — hør du
good græshus — gode gud

Svigermor maa bide i Græsset.

1. "Does your wife have visitors today, Ola?" "It sounds that way."

2. "I wonder what's wrong." "There's an awful racket."

3. "I've been thinking for a long time, Mari, of giving you a piece of my mind, and now you're going to get it, too." "Oh, horrors!"

4. "You needn't think you can be the boss here in my house — I know that much anyway."

En mislykket Prøve.

1. "So you've got this new machine in running order, Per." "Oh sure, I've got the steam up, too, so we can test it."

2. "Let 'er go!"

3. "Shall I pull or push this lever, Per?" "You have to push it first, just like this."

4. "Ow! Ow!"

---

ein piece ov my mind — en god overhaling
bas — mester, bas

rønning order — i kjøreklar stand
steam — damp
let 'er go — la 'o gå
lever'n — stanga

1. "What in the world is wrong, Per?" "Jupiter is stuck in a mud hole."

2. "Oh, this job is not difficult at all. I saw many cases like it in New York."

3. "Now all together — one two —"

4. "— three."

1. "Hol' on, hol' on, don't walk into the mud puddle there."

2. "I'll find a stone to step on, Polla."

3. "It isn't necessary for you to muddy your shoes."

4. "This will be better."

ætaal — slett (ikke)
now all together — nå alle sammen

hol' an — stopp

1. "Have you thought any more about the trip to the North Pole, Per?" "Yeah sure. I ordered two airplanes the other day." "Per, come and take away the cat here."

2. "But do you think we can get ready in time to join Amundsen?" "No, that will be pretty tight, but —" "Mee-ow-ow"

3. "You see, we can leave later." "Mee-ow-ow." "Ow! Ow! Watch what you're doing, Per!"

1. "What's the matter with the old woman today, Per?" "Oh, she's complaining about this bent finger. I wonder if something couldn't be done about it."

2. "If I could straighten it out again, I think it would get better." "Well that ought to be possible."

3. "Ouch! ouch!" "See there!"

4. "Sic 'em there!"

---

sjur — sjølsagt
æroplaner — fly

Roald Amundsen fløy over det arktiske område med Lincoln Ellsworth uten å nå Nordpolen i 1925

streit'en — rette den (ut)
sic 'em there — puss ta dem

Et uventet Resultat.

1. "Haw haw! My, how little you know!"   **2.** "I know a better trick, Ola."   **3.** "See, there it comes." "I've never seen anything like it."

Svigermor faar en uventet Bekomst.

1. "I should have split up some kindling wood before I leave, but Ola is out here waiting." "Mamma says she can do it."   **2.** "Tra la la —"   **3.** "—la la—"

---

trik — knep   *splitte* — kløvd

1. "Don't you think, Ola, that we should organize a club for the prevention of cruelty to animals? I think it is so awful to see how animals—"

2. "—get mistreated."

3. "I'll teach you, you swine!"

4. "Yes, you're quite right about what you said, Per — ha ha ha."

1. "The mules are well enough, but I think they're awfully slow." "Oh, they are perhaps a little slow, but then you don't need to be afraid you're going to have a runaway. They're not afraid of anything whatever."

2. "And not only that, but they are much tougher than a horse team." "You may be right about that."

3. "Hold the reins tight!" "Whoa back! Whoa back!"

4. "Whoa! Whoa!" "Hang on to the reins!" "Wait a minute, Per, here I have food and coffee."

---

for the Prevention of Cruelty to Animals — mot dyremishandling
mistrita — mishandla

mjuladn — muldyrene
slo — seine
rønævei — at hestene blir løpske

hesteteam — hestespann
ho bæk — ptro

1. "Well, today both the airplanes I ordered have come, Ola." "You don't say. Then we'd better test them, too."

2. "It seems to run all right." "Yes, you bet!"

3. "How do you feel, Per?" "Oh my, this is fine."

4. "What shall we do now, Ola?" "Don't you have another airplane, too?"

Ola og Per paa Vei til Nordpolen — Ola and Per on Their Way to the North Pole   197

1. "Look, Ola, there we have the Arctic Ocean." "No, Per, that's Lake Superior."

2. "Stop! Stop! I lost something."

æroplæner'a — flyene
testa — prøvd
oh my, dis is fine — ja dette er flott

The Arctic Ocean — Nordishavet
Lake Superior — Øvresjøen

1. "But Per, we have to start for home. We have only three crackers and half a sausage left, and now bleak winter is starting." "You can leave, Ola. I for my part am through with the world. I have nothing to live for any more."

2. "Well well, goodbye then, Per. I'm going back home to Mari."

3. "Woof!" "Uff!!"

4. "Ola! Ola! You're not going to leave me here, are you, you confounded nitwit!"

1. "Look, there's Amundsen's airplane, Per!" "Well, by thunder!"

2. "It's entirely O.K., too!" "And it isn't frozen down, either!"

3. "Hurrah, Ola! Now we've cleared the ice!"

4. "I guess it'll be best we set our course to Canada, Per?" "Yes, sure."

baund te — nødt til å
crackers — kjeks
gudbai — farvel
leave — etterlate

cleara — kommet klar av
ja sjur — ja visst

Per paa Eskimojagt

1. "This could have been a real disaster, Per." "Oh, I've seen worse things, Ola."

2. "You better start a fire, and I'll look around to see if anybody lives here." "Where am I going to find wood?"

3. "Wake up, Per! I met two Eskimo girls, and they —"

4. "Where are they at?"

En Pølsestub for en Ford

1. "Hey fellow! Now we're saved, Per! I traded that piece of sausage I had for this new model Ford from an Eskimo."

2. "It seems to be knocking a little." "Well, you see, it should have been overhauled."

3. "Look, there's the name of a town. Now we'll soon be in civilization again!" "Well, I'll be darned!!"

4. "Hol' on!"

ein feir — ild, varme
wake up — vågn opp

knocker — banker, støter
overhaala — overhala

straight ahead — rett fram
sharp turn — skarp sving

1. "What'll we do now, Ola?" "Oh, we'll put it on top of this iceberg here, and then we'll drag the whole business over to the shore."

2. "Is that far enough, Per?" "We'll have to pull it up on the edge, here."

3. "Push it back, Per. It's tipping over."

Fordens sidste Reis

1. "I can't get it started. It must have lost compression." "In that case, I suppose I have to go back and hunt for it."

2. "Wait a minute, Per. I think we're out of gas, man."

3. "I'll strike a match, so you can see, Ola."

---

isberge — isflaket, isfjellet
tipper over — velter

compression — kompresjon, trykk
  (i sylindrene)

ute taa — sloppet opp for
gas — bensin

1. "We're soon in Alaska now, Per, so I think we'll make it after all."

2. "What's the matter now, again?" "Oh, I have such a stomach ache!"

3. "Ouch, ouch, Ola!"

4. "Where did you go, Per?"
Skiltet: Til Alaska, 200 miles (35 norske mil)

Finder Andrees Ballon, som forsvandt for 30 Aar siden
They Find Andrée's Balloon, Lost 30 Years Ago 205

1. "Well, by jiminy, there's Andrée's balloon!" "I've never seen the like! I wonder if it's usable?"

2. "Is it all right, Ola?" "It's absolutely sound, man. Keep the fire going."

3. "Now you have to be quick, Per, and grab hold of the basket when we cut the rope. One — two — three — go!"

4. "Stop, stop, you fool!"

---

mæka de' — klare det
bai jimini — du store verden

Andrée — svensk polarforsker (1854—1897, som prøvde uten hell å fly over nordpolen i ballong; hans lik ble funnet i 1930)

sound — i god stand
keep the feier going — hold varmen ved like
bæsketen — kurven, gondolen

2. "Go ahead, Ola, jump on this net and we will save you."

3. "Here I come!"

4. "Gosh!"

1. "Well, how did you get to St. Paul, Per?" "Oh, I got here by train from Winnipeg."

2. "But how did you get to Winnipeg?" "Oh, never mind."

3. "Well, let that be as it may. We're safe now." "Yes, now we're safe."

4. "I almost think we were safer on the North Pole, man!" "Yeah, you bet!"

Montgomery Ward and Co. —kjent postordrefirma
St. Paul — hovedstad i delstaten Minnesota

go ahead osv. — kjør på, Ola, og hopp på dette nettet, vi skal redde deg
gosh — jøsses

treine — toget
never meind — aldri bry deg
safe — trygg
safar — tryggere

ju bet — det skal være visst
Winnipeg — by i den kanadiske provinsen Manitoba

Eu uheldig Isseilads

1. "You surely haven't intended to ride on the Mississippi River from St. Paul to La Crosse on something like that, have you?" "It'll go fast, you'll see, in this strong north wind."

2. "Now you can hoist the sail, Per, and then I'll steer." "Here she goes."

3. "Hol' on, Ola, not so fast!"

4. "Stop, Ola, are you crazy?" "Let down the sail, you fool!"

Seiladsen faar en brat Afslutning

1. "Lower the sail, Per. Now we're at La Crosse!" "Oh, just let it go, I'm done for anyway."

2. "Can't you hear that we must stop, Per! We're soon at Davenport!" "Oh, let it go."

3. "Good land! Stop, stop, Per! Now we're at the end of the ice!" "Oh, just let it go."

4. "Stop! Stop!" "Oh, just let it go."

Læcrosse — by i delstaten Wisconsin på Mississippi-elven
here she goes — nå går den

gone — slått ut
Davenport — by i delstaten Iowa
good land — herregud

Blir taget for farlige Folk.

1. "Say you, can you show us the way home?" "Where do you live?" "It's hard to explain that. We're not like other folks, we're sort of imaginary—"

2. "Yes, I can understand that!"

3. "Gee whiz!"

4. "I don't dare let fellows like that walk around loose here." "Hey, there!"

Lars "gaar igjen"

1. "Well, now we've got a hole in the ice." "We most certainly have that."

2. "Your fingers get cold today." "You can no doubt say that."

3. "Pfui!"

explæne — forklare
imaginære — fantasifostre
gee whiz — jøsses
hey there — hei du

Lake Superior — Øvresjøen

1. "What in the world does this mean?"

2. "Ladies and gentlemen! Let me explain — "

3. "Stop, stop! Now listen to me — "

4. "You contemptible barbarian!!"

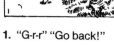

1. "G-r-r" "Go back!"

2. "Oh no! Oh no!"

ladies and gentlemans — mine damer og herrer
explæne — forklare

go back — gå tilbake

1. "I'm getting awfully hungry, Ola." "Me too. We'd better stop in at a farmer's and ask for some food."

2. "Good morning ma'm! We're so hungry. Can we have ein bite?" "Sure Mike!"

3. "Sic 'em!"

4. "Ola! Ola!" "There you are."

1. "But we can't let ourselves starve to death, Ola. If I don't misremember, it says that it is not a sin to steal when it is a deed of necessity." "Yes, darned if it doesn't!"

2. "Sh-h! I can't get hold of them." "Wait a minute, Per."

3. "Can you reach them now?" "Yeah, you bet!"

---

farmer — bonde
God morgen, frue! Vi er så sultne. Kan vi få en bit?

sure Mike — ja det er sikkert
there you are — der fikk du det
sic 'em — puss ta dem

ja ju bet — ja visst

1. "I can't stand to walk any farther, Ola. If you get home again, bring Polla my greetings and tell her that I was thinking of her to the very end." "Well well, as you wish. I'll cover you over with straw, so you don't freeze to death."

2. "Goodbye, Ola. Thanks for everything." "Oh shucks."

4. "Ouch, ouch, Ola! Are you crazy?"

1. "It was about time you got back home, you confounded heathen!" "Not so fast, Værmor —"

2. "Now you better tend to that screaming brat of yours!"

3. "Brat!? Brat!?" "Don't you know that Polla has gotten a baby?"

4. "Well, now we'll see something!"

---

covre de op — dekke over deg
straa — halm
aa shucks — å tøys

tende te — passe, stelle
bebi — barn, unge

1. "Are you going to town, Per?" "Yes, I have to go to the depot to pick up a C.O.D. package from Duluth."

2. "Is there something for me?" "Yes, sir— Fifty dollars, please."

3. "There it is."

4. "Are you totally crazy, Lars?" "No, you see, I ran short of cash, and so I thought it would be a good idea to come by C.O.D. express."

1. "Hello, Doctor. Welcome back — hee, hee." "How do you do, Madam, heh — heh."

2. "What do you have in your jug?"

3. "It's just black molasses — I thought —"

4. "You can't fool me!"

---

depon — stasjonen
C.O.D. — som fraktgods (betalt ved ankomsten)
Duluth — by i delstaten Minnesota

is der somting for mei — er det noe til meg
there it is — der er det

rønna short av cash — slapp opp for kontanter
express — ilgods

juggen din — krukken din
malasi — (tykk, mørk) sirup
fule — narre

1. "Per! Per! The soot is burning!"

2. "What are you going to use the dynamite for, Per?" "Mind your own business!"

3. "I know what I'm doing, Værmor. I saw them using dynamite to put out an awful fire in St. Paul last fall."

1. "Have you been able to rent a new place, Per?" "Yes, sure. I've rented a section of land in Dakota. We're moving today."

2. "It's terrible how much stuff we have with us, Per." "Nobody knows how much they have until they're going to move, Polla."

3. "Per! Per! Where's the baby?" "By jiminy! I forgot and left it behind, Polla!"

4. "We've forgotten the child!"

---

meind your own biznes — legg deg ikke borti dette
feir — brann
plads — gård

ja sjur — javisst
ein section — et jordstykke på 640 acres, omtrent 2500 mål

move — flytte
bai jimini — herregud

En slem Forglemmelse

1. "Can't you find the baby, Polla?" "Oh no, oh no! Boo-hoo-hoo-" "I've never seen anything like it." "Isn't he upstairs then, Polla?"

2. "Don't cry so, Polla, boo-hoo—" "Oh Per, oh Per!" "Boo-hoo-oo-oo" "Da da."

3. "Well, I'll be darned! Now I know where the child is at — I put it down in a bureau drawer."

Naar Enden er god, er alting godt

1. "I think they must have gone absolutely mad!"

2. "Where's the bureau at, Per?" "Oh, that's right. It was left over by the house wall."

4. "Da da."

---

opstærs — ovenpå, på loftet
bureau — kommode

bjuron — kommoden

The numerical order is that of the publication of the comic strips in *Decorah-Posten*. The R number after the title is that given by Rosendahl when he began to number each comic strip. The volume number and page number refer to the reprint in one of the eight published collections.

1918

19 February	1. Da han Ola fik den nye «Karsen»
16 April	2. Per og Ola paa Skunkefangst. I, 5
26 April	3. Vær venlig mod Dyrene. I, 13
28 May	4. Per paa Frierfærd. En sørgelig historie om, naar man tar feil af Vinduerne. I, 7
2 August	5. Per og Ola «fixer» Purka
13 December	6. Slagtedag paa Farmen. I, 9

1919

| 18 March | 7. Per og Ola paa Ulvejagt. I, 47 |

1920

9 January	8. «Paa Ridestellet skal Storfolk kjendes,» sa Ola til Kjæringen om Ford'en hendes. I, 3
16 January	9. Naar en kan snakke Yeinki. I, 15
23 January	10. «En lærer saa længe en lever.» I, 31
13 February	11. Han Per skal «borde teacher'n.» I, 43
30 April	12. Per optræder som Maskin-Expert. I, 45b
6 May	13. En brydsom Kalv — og en uventet Modtagelse. I, 45a
14 May	14. Per opdager «det svage Kjøns svageste Side.» I, 19b
2 July	15. Det er aldrig saa galt at det ikke kunde gaaet værre. I, 35a
3 September	16. Da Fortjenesten sprang i Luften. I, 19a
17 September	17. Eika brast og hele Stasen gik i Vasken. I, 29b
1 October	18. Per «topper ta» Stakken. I, 11a
26 October	19. Da Per skulde «fixe Blowern.» I, 11b
5 November	20. Lars finder ud hvad «slo» betyder i Amerika. I, 33a
19 November	21. Per kommer i en slem Knibe. I, 21b
26 November	22. Ola faar et «Sørpreisparty.» I, 21a
3 December	23. En uventet Medhjælper. I, 25b
10 December	24. Per finder Vand ved hjælp af Ønskekvisten. I, 17a
17 December	25. Per skiller sig af med en Kjær Ven. I, 37a
24 December	26. Et næsevist Svin. I, 37b
31 December	27. Per gaar paa Frierfod. I, 29a

1921

7 January	28. Nykommeren Lars' Gjenvordigheder. I, 33b
14 January	29. Per «retter Smed for Bager,» eller Kua som fik undgjælde for Grisen. I, 39a
21 January	30. En pudsig Rottefangst. I, 27a
28 January	31. Per er aldrig hjælpeløs! I, 27b

4 February	32. Et probat Middel mod Bog-Agenter. I, 39b
11 February	33. Per gir Bul'n en Lærepenge. I, 23a
18 February	34. Per foretar en uventet Luftreise. I, 23b
25 February	35. Da han Ola skulde snyte Dentistad'n. I, 41a
4 March	36. Per og Ola paa Vei til Statefæra. I, 35b
11 March	37. Per «fixer» Høiforken. I, 25a
18 March	38. Et uventet Besøg — Per drar tilskogs. I, 17b
7 October	39. Per og Ola faar en «Surpris». II, 3a
14 October	40. Den kalven var ikke saa «luset»! II, 13b
21 October	41. Det er ikke greit at være Nykommer, sier'n Lars. II, 35b
28 October	42. Per kommer i en Klemme. II, 23a
4 November	43. Nykommeren Lars holder i «Taumadn.» II, 35a
11 November	44. Den som ler sidst ler ofte bedst. I, 41b
18 November	45. Han blev sint han Per. II, 13a
25 November	46. Han er aldrig «ebeita» han Per. II, 11a
2 December	47. Per og Ola «tester» Brua. II, 23b
9 December	48. Lars og «Kæt» kommer ikke rigtig godt overens. II, 45b
16 December	49. Lars og «Potet Buggen.» II, 29b
23 December	50. Ja, det forandrer Sagen. II, 19b
30 December	51. Da Ola skulde stelle hjemme. II, 11b

1922

6 January	52. Per og Ola paa Bjørnejagt. II, 45a
13 January	53. Ola «kurerer» Hesten hans Per. II, 19a
20 January	54. Per viser Ola hvor «smart» han er. II, 29a
27 January	55. «Kaunting» som Middel mod Søvnløshed. II, 37b
3 February	56. Per prøver de nye «Styregreier.» II, 39a
10 February	57. Paa Jagt efter «Moonshiners.» II, 37a
17 February	58. The Engine is «missing.» II, 33b
24 February	59. Per er en «Klypper» til at koge Graut. II, 41b
3 March	60. Lars tar feil af Situationen. II, 41a
10 March	61. Da Per og Ola skulde lage «Gigtmelesin.» II, 33a
17 March	62. Per demonstrerer for Ola «Safety First.» II, 39b
24 March	63. Per har faaet vondt i Benet. II, 5a
31 March	64. Ola og Per laver en Molbohistorie. II, 5b
7 April	65. Per ved Raad for Uraad. II, 27b
14 April	66. Nu maa en da endelig bli kvit denne Purka. II, 15a
21 April	67. Per er en dugelig «Faiermand.» II, 27a
28 April	68. «Kate» er altid den samme Vrangpeis. II, 17b
5 May	69. Per er ingen Damernes Ven. II, 25a
12 May	70. Per faar skjæmt ud Øksen paa Fillehue hans Ola. II, 43a
19 May	71. Lars faar sig et «Sørpræisparti» paa Nakken. II, 31b
26 May	72. Lars finder ud at Vandet er vaadt. II, 43b